Shaking Down Santa

Susan Law Corpany

Hand over the milk and cookies and nobody gets hurt.

Lauren Baylor is still reeling from the loss of her husband who died while deployed in Afghanistan. Unsure if she's even ready to date again, she is focused on trying to normalize things for her children. Her life and her holiday season become further complicated as she finds herself pursued romantically by two men wearing Santa suits.

Police sergeant Bryan Everett, drafted by his sister to play Santa for the young neighborhood widow and her two little boys, overcomes his reluctance when he meets the beautiful Lauren. In the days ahead, Bryan tries to help Lauren through her grief, hoping that someday his patience will pay off.

Meanwhile, Lauren has also caught the attention of Lloyd Owens, a divorced father with custody of his two little girls. Not to be outdone, the overzealous suitor scores a Santa suit of his own, dilapidated though it may be, and sets out to show Lauren that he can be the answer to all her problems . . . or the beginning of some new ones.

When disturbing phone calls and a home intrusion rock her world, Lauren isn't sure who to turn to or trust. Is Bryan a crooked cop? Or is Lloyd, the devoted father and faithful churchgoer, leading a double life? Upheaval, intrigue and unwelcome romantic attentions are *not* what she wanted for Christmas.

Dedicated to those soldiers
who gave their all
And to the women
Who soldier on without them

Acknowledgements

First, I want to thank my friend Anita Sacre for inspiring the title of this book by trying to brighten the Christmas of a young widow and her little boy decades ago by sending over her brother to play Santa. I turned him away because I didn't recognize him as anyone I knew. He reported back to his sister that I "shook him down." For the record, I stopped short of a strip search (although now that I think about it "Strip Searching Santa" has even more alliteration), but yeah, I wasn't going to invite some strange Santa into my home. A reminder of that unsuccessful Santa visit was all it took to get my creative juices flowing. Add in some memories of a fellow single parent and blind date who was ready to propose before I was halfway through my prime rib on the first date, some disturbing phone calls from a strange man, and another novel novel is born. And to Anita's brother, the hapless Santa, whoever and wherever you may be, I'm sorry!

Thanks also to my many friends and family members who read through this book in its formative stages. I can't remember all of you, but I appreciate your assistance. If I name names, I will surely forget someone. When I've got all these made-up people living in my head, they sometimes crowd out the real ones who should be there. Many eagle-eyed proofreaders and nitpickers are always welcome. My stepdaughter Becky and my daughter-in-law Zaneta were especially helpful with their comments and corrections. Thanks to my friend Ann Allred, who caught several things I missed. Jean, thanks as always for your unwavering support and for giving the book to all your family members for Christmas. I'm glad at least a couple of them arrived just in the St. Nick of time. (I was able to remember all of these people's names because I have tangible physical evidence of their help, so in the future, if you want to be remembered by name, leave something I can see and your chances will vastly improve.)

I would like to especially thank Debra Erfert, who was the spokesperson for her husband, Mike, my go-to guy for questions about police work. Any law enforcement stuff I got right is because of their help. (Anything I messed up, I did myself.) I would also like to thank my friendly neighborhood police officer down at Kealakekua Bay who let me sit in one of the chairs usually occupied by the locals while I picked his brain. I've forgotten his name, but I didn't forget his help. Thanks as well to my friend Shelley Locke's husband, Mr. Shelley Locke, who answered all my law enforcement questions over dinner in Honolulu. Thanks to the military guy at the bed and breakfast in Oregon who answered my questions over the breakfast buffet.

Much gratitude is due to Annette Lyon for introducing me to the concept of "Flat Daddies" (and for giving me the idea for chapter fourteen). As I pondered the idea of cardboard parents for kids whose parents are deployed, I could not help but wonder what happens when Dad or Mom doesn't come home and the cardboard parent is all a child has left.

Author friend Roseanne Wilkins held my hand every step of the way bringing the e-book and paperback to life, juggling the challenges of a large and ever-expanding family and applying her expertise and experience on my behalf. A few more books and maybe I'll figure out how to do some of this stuff for myself.

Much gratitude is also due to Candace Salima, another woman I'm convinced secretly sports a shirt with an "S" on the front, or would if there were still phone booths around in which to make the transformation to Superhero. When Candace told me she was looking for a novel to serialize during December on her new website, newscornerusa.com, and I had a Christmas novel with 31 chapters, I didn't have to think about it very long.

Saved for last is my long-suffering husband Thom who puts up with the hazards of being the spouse of a writer—long periods of neglect, rushed meals and wrinkled clothes, providing therapy for fictional characters. He has all the tools of the trade—a spatula for scraping me up off the pavement when I become discouraged, a cattle prod to keep me moving forward, a sense of humor, a professorial knowledge of just about everything, the patience of Job, and an ability to love unconditionally and forgive readily. (And he hates my run-on sentences.) My greatest success as a writer is the book that I wrote that helped me win his heart. If I never make another dime as a writer, I have been paid back in spades.

Contents

Contents

Chapter One

Too soon

Lauren Baylor pushed her green beans around on her plate, wishing she had not allowed her friend Charlene to talk her into a date with her brother, not this soon after Kendall's death. Although almost a year-and-a-half had passed, that first year had been a blur of difficult decisions and changes forced upon her by unwelcome circumstances. In the last few months she had finally started to feel she was beginning to come to terms with her new reality, but she was still uncertain if she wanted the additional complications sure to come with socializing and dating.

She closed her eyes momentarily, recalling a snapshot of her old life, but when she opened them it was not Kendall looking lovingly at her across their dining room table; it was a virtual stranger staring at her across a table at Outback Steakhouse. She tried to tell herself that it was good to get out and spend an evening in the company of another adult, albeit one she didn't know and wasn't sure she liked, and who seemed to be single-handedly devouring the Bloomin' Onion that was supposed to be a shared appetizer. Lloyd Owens smiled at her across the table. "Charlene says you have two little boys."

"Yes, Brett is two-and-a-half and Dirk is four, almost five."

He grinned. "Perfect! My girls are six and eight."

He reached across the table, looking as if he were going to take her hand that had been resting beside her plate. She jerked back her hand instinctively, almost upending her glass of cranberry juice in the process. He studied her quietly.

"Sorry, it was rude of me to reach. Would you mind passing the salt?"

Embarrassed, she silently handed him the salt shaker, located close to where her hand had been.

"I'm not much for spicy foods. Salt and pepper are about all I ever put on my food. I have a sensitive stomach," Lloyd said.

Are we going to talk about our intestinal woes now? Your sensitive stomach hasn't slowed you down on inhaling our appetizer. Lauren searched for another safe topic of conversation. "So how are your girls adjusting to school here? Boulder has some pretty good schools."

"Oh, it's always hard to be the new kid, but they're adjusting, making friends, keeping up. Divorce is hard on kids, and adding a move on top of it doesn't help. Tell me about your little boys."

She pulled a couple of pictures out of her wallet and pushed them across the table.

He picked up the pictures and looked at them. "So the little one is blondish like you. Does he have your beautiful green eyes, too?"

She ignored the compliment. "His eyes are blue."

"Did your older son get his red hair from his father?"

Blondish. Must mean I'm overdue to have my highlights redone. "I've got a brother with red hair, and yes, Kendall was a redhead, so Dirk got it from both sides of the family."

As he studied the pictures, she felt a sudden unexplainable urge to grab them and put them safely back in her wallet once again.

Mom's right. I really am a helicopter mother. She had recently removed all the pictures of her boys from her Facebook account and had "defriended" anyone who was not personally known to her. She had kept all the ladies from the church book club who were her personal friends but the "friends of friends" who had joined the online book discussion group were history. Kendall's death had left her as the sole protector of her sons. You could never be too careful.

She reached across the table and retrieved the pictures. "Dirk is in preschool, and he seems to enjoy that. Before his last deployment, Kendall gave us some cardboard cutouts he had made of himself so the boys would be able to remember him and feel like he was around. One of them is from the waist up only, so it can ride in the car and go places with us. He's become very attached to that one. We call him 'Half-Daddy.' Anyway, everyone thought it was really cute that he wanted to take his cardboard daddy with him everywhere . . . until Kendall died. Then suddenly it seemed to be a very disturbing behavior, even though he isn't doing anything different than he was before."

"Can't you lose it, like the security blanket that gets lost between the washer and the dryer?"

At the look she gave him, he quickly swallowed a bite of prime rib and posed another question. "And your youngest?"

"Brett is a sweet, quiet little guy. My mother is very concerned that he's not talking much, but he comprehends what I say to him. Frankly, my mother-in-law is much more help, so I'm glad she's nearby. She says he has an old soul and she always comments on how bright and observant he seems. At a time like this I really don't need anybody pointing out negatives to me."

"Sure, but if something is really wrong, you don't want to miss it."

"Sometimes not talking can be a good thing." She shoveled a huge bite of mashed potatoes into her mouth. *Some people talk way too much. Like why am I telling this guy all about my kids? It isn't like I plan to see him again.*

"So are you close to them?"

"My *kids*?"

"No, your in-laws."

"Oh, yes. Very close. They've been great through this whole thing. They live closer than my parents. I moved here to be close to them. We were in military housing in Fort Collins, but when you're no longer a military spouse, they don't give you much time before you have to move."

"That's harsh."

"It felt that way, but what are they supposed to do? There are others waiting for housing, and they don't really want you around as a reminder to other military wives of what could happen to them. It was hard to be uprooted from that built-in support system, so I moved close to his parents where I knew I'd have lots of help."

"It would seem you would be more likely to move closer to your own family."

3

"His parents are my family, too. Staying in Colorado just seemed like the most logical thing to do. Boulder was his home town. There are people here who will help my sons to know who their father was. That's important to me. I'm especially close to Janet, my mother-in-law. She's the one person I feel truly understands my loss."

"I understand your husband is a big hero, around here."

She gave him another studied look, wondering if he meant that comment in the "big-fish-in-a-small-pond" way it sounded.

"He was a Combat Medical Specialist. I'm sure if he were here, he would say he was just doing his job, doing what he had been trained to do, tend to the wounded. People have called him fearless, but I have decided there probably isn't such a thing as a fearless soldier. There are just people who push on through the fear or don't allow it to register. Yes, now he's a hero. But he was already a hero in my eyes."

"*I'm* sure if he were here, he'd say, 'Hey buddy, what are you doing having dinner with my wife?'"

"*That's* what you got from that explanation?" Lauren asked.

"Sure, he's a hero. I googled him, read some of the articles. That's some tough competition. Your ex rescued what was it, three wounded men that day, before he stepped on . . ."

She choked on the most recent swallow of her juice. Trying her best to be civil, she spoke slowly and firmly. "Please do not call him 'my ex.' *You* are the one with an 'ex.'" *And while you're at it, if you have a sensitive bone in your body, please, please, please, don't make me relive it all yet another time by rehearsing the details.*

"I meant 'ex' as in former." He continued to make his case. "Is he still here?"

"That isn't the point. 'Ex' is a derogatory term." *This is a lost cause. I should just shut up and chew faster and this whole evening will be behind me sooner.*

"I'm sorry. I wasn't thinking. I shouldn't generalize my feelings towards my ex. You *obviously* still care about your husband," Lloyd said.

Even his apology is annoying. He says that like I'm going to stop loving Kendall one of these days. If this is what dating is going to be like, count me out.

"I mean what kind of woman just runs off and leaves two adorable little girls without a mother? Her job was always more important to her than her children, but when she got that big promotion in another city, that was all the excuse she needed to leave us all, without so much as a backward glance. She no longer wanted to be encumbered by her family on her way up to shatter the glass ceiling."

Lauren studied the man across the table, wondering momentarily if she was being as insensitive to his situation as he was being to hers. Lloyd wasn't bad looking, she supposed. He had dark close-cropped curly hair and pleasant-enough features. He didn't have much of tan for someone who had just moved from Florida, but she supposed that was an occupational hazard of an office job. He wasn't tall, but he was tall enough. He wasn't quite as trim as he could be, but again office jobs did that to a person, she supposed. From when they had walked side by side into the restaurant, she'd judged he had maybe an inch on her. She had gotten used to towering over boys in middle school, but eventually most of them had caught up and eventually surpassed her in height. She imagined that if his personality wasn't so grating, she might be able to find herself somewhat physically attracted to him.

"So you have full custody?" she asked.

"Possession is nine-tenths of the law, as they say. Not that I didn't have to ultimately fight for custody. Yes, the girls are all mine now and we are a family in search of a mother."

For the second time that evening, Lauren choked while trying to swallow. "Lloyd, your sister mentioned this was your first date after your divorce. Lines like that, well they tend to send a woman running for the hills."

"Not if she's the *right* woman," he beamed.

Well, I'm headed straight for Pike's Peak. "Okay, I'm confused. She left you but you had to fight for custody? Couldn't you just charge her with abandonment or something?"

5

"It's complicated. She left but then once she got settled, she tried to get custody, tried to use her increased wealth as leverage. She took the money she got from our house and . . ."

"You were able to sell your house that quickly in a depressed market?" Lauren asked.

"Oh, we didn't sell. I refinanced and cashed her out for her half of the equity. Anyway, so she put that down on a big beautiful house in Atlanta. Homes are really reasonable there, especially compared to where we were in Boca Raton, in south Florida. Then I used up most of the rest of my equity paying lawyers to fight for custody. I won, but then I got laid off from my job at Motorola and had to do a short sale on my beautiful lakeside home, was lucky at that point not to be underwater on it. But I suppose that's what you get for buying waterfront." He chuckled at his little joke, until he noticed he was laughing alone.

Okay, so I'm not the only one who has gone through hard times. Maybe I've been a little hard on the guy. Perhaps this isn't the time to mention that I got my house here on a short-sale. "Wow! That sounds like a rough year."

"So anyway, that's how we ended up here, with me working construction for my brother-in-law, living in a cramped apartment, and grateful for the goodwill of my sister and her husband. She's my step-sister actually. And I'm sorry if I came on too strong. I do that. With the holidays and all, I can't help but want things to be different, to want that traditional family, for my daughters to have a mom around baking cookies with them and stuff like that. But the important thing is that I've got my little girls and they're safe and happy." He smiled, trying one more time to reach for her hand. "But the nicest thing my sister has done for me so far is introduce me to you."

It was difficult for her, but Lauren did not draw back her hand when he put his on top of hers. She suspected he had made up the story that he had been reaching for the salt shaker previously. She wondered if he would notice that her ring finger had a fresh indent. She was sure he had no idea how heart-wrenchingly difficult it had been for her to remove her wedding ring for this date. He would also likely never know that she was planning to go right back home

6

and put it on again. It was all she could do not to draw back her hand because it felt so foreign to have another man touching her. She felt sorry for this man who had obviously been through so much and was so out of touch with how to proceed on a date, who had made no secret of his interest in her, but no matter what anyone else thought about the timing, it was too soon. It was simply too soon.

Chapter Two

The Update

Charlene Hamilton reached for a roll of wrapping paper and instructed her step-brother, Lloyd. "Okay, I'll wrap. You tape." She cut a wide piece of silver paper. "Smoldering looks, you say? On the first date?"

"Oh yeah, but not the good kind. I totally blew it, several times. That's why I need the perspective of a woman. I have a good feeling about Lauren, Char. Of course, she's still getting over her husband who died, but she's too young not to move on. In spite of all that, I think there was a definite vibe. This may not seem like a big deal, but by the end of the dinner, she let me take her hand, across the table, and it was electric. Who could have ever thought I could get such a jolt simply from holding hands. And get this. Her little boys are two and four and my girls are six and eight."

"Perfect! It's as if you were meant for each other."

"Exactly! That's what I thought, too," Lloyd said. "After Amber, I so want the girls to have a stable mother figure. I could tell just hearing Lauren talk about her little boys that she's a devoted mother. She'd never put a career and a promotion ahead of her family."

"I hate to see you and the girls stuck in that dinky apartment over the holidays. Why don't you stay here in our basement?" She smiled conspiratorially. "It would be more homey *and* you'd be closer to Lauren."

"Really?" He perked up at this suggestion. "You don't mind? Don't you need to discuss it with Ryan?"

"Oh, he does what I tell him to do. He hired you on at the construction firm, even though things are slow this time of year, didn't he?"

"I was surprised when he agreed to pay me under the table. It will help a lot for me to get on my feet if I don't have to pay taxes right now."

"Short term, sure. Until you find something better. He wasn't happy about that. He's pretty much of a straight arrow, especially when it comes to his business, but I told him how you spent your last dime fighting for custody of the girls, and he finally softened. I'll let you in on a little secret. Not many people know this. Ryan's firm was pretty much on the brink of collapse with the economy like it is. When my dad died, he left everything to me, me being his only child. He didn't leave anything to my mother or your mother or the lady he married after that. You know what they say. 'Many a man owes his success to his first wife and his second wife to his success.' Dad never could run a marriage very well, but he was a great businessman, probably because he paid more attention to his business than to his wife of the moment."

"He left it *all* to you? I wish my father would have agreed to let him adopt me when he wanted to."

"Yeah, I bet you do." She laughed. "Anyway, I sold his businesses, all but one, for a good profit, kept the same guy on who had been running it for years. I know nothing about what they do really, but I admit I love going down there and having everyone go 'It's the owner!' and quake in their boots. I've been able to make some good investments on the side, and I wasn't only able to pull Ryan's company back from the brink of bankruptcy, but I invested enough in it to make it one of the most successful construction companies in the Denver area, maybe even all of Colorado."

"I'm impressed." Lloyd hesitated. "I feel like such a loser, descending on you, broke and out of work, but you know I really would have paid my last dime to my lawyer to get custody of the girls. I'm thankful I didn't lose my job until the custody battle was over. I could very well have lost the home. I escaped foreclosure by a hair. Unemployed Dad versus Mom with big advancement in her career could have toppled it in the other direction quite easily." He looked heavenward. "I'll tell you what, Charlene. Someone up there was looking out for me, all through this. There were so many miracles and . . ." His voice caught. "You've been so good to me. I just hope I don't look like a freeloader."

"Nonsense! In the first place, so many people are out of work right now, there's almost no shame in that anymore. And in the

10

second place, you're an awesome dad who did battle for your little girls. Not to take anything away from Kendall Baylor, but you're a hero, too."

"Do you think Lauren could ever see me that way?"

"I don't know, but I'll certainly do whatever I can to help." She topped the silver package with a midnight-blue bow. "Don't worry, Phil . . ." she stopped herself. "I mean Lloyd. I can't help but want to call you Phillip. So tell me again why you're going by your middle name."

"I just got so tired of being little Phil. I wanted my own name, my own identity," he said.

"Yeah, Phillip Lloyd Owens, Junior. I guess that was a lot to live up to. Maybe that's part of why he didn't want my dad to adopt you. I wonder how all that would have worked when my dad and your mom split."

"Same as if I was his kid, I guess. The custody battles, all that." He paused. "I know it doesn't compare to what she has endured, but maybe sometime I can tell Lauren about all I went through to keep my girls safe. It wasn't just the issue of Amber's job. Imagine picking up your little girls from their mother and hearing about her *sleepovers*." He shook his head. "How could I hope to have them grow up with any kind of morals when their mother had a different man over every weekend? These days you have to be careful about even bringing up moral issues. I'm grateful I got a conservative judge."

"Me, too. I'm sure it helped that you could demonstrate a record as a faithful churchgoer." She paused. "Wait. How did you do weekend visits? Didn't you say earlier that you were in Florida and she was in Atlanta?"

"Oh, we were separated for a time, and she got an apartment nearby, while we fought for custody."

"That makes sense. Yeah, you never know in these liberal times if the religion thing is going to backfire, if you might pull a judge who is sleeping with the court reporter and is going to see you as a self-righteous right-wing nut job," Charlene said.

"Too true. That's how I registered last election."

11

She laughed. "That *should* be a party." She reached over and gave him a hug. "I'll try to remember on the name, but you'll always be little Phillip to me. I was so sad when Dad and Jackie broke up. You were my baby brother. You were two when they got married, and what, ten when they divorced? I hated being an only child. I cried and cried when you went away, especially when I understood that you weren't going to visit on the weekends. I'm so glad you found me."

"It wasn't that hard. What would we do without the Internet?"

"I know you're only my step-brother but if you need anything else . . ."

"Technically, I'm your *ex-step-brother,* but who's keeping track?" Lloyd paused. "So I made the mistake of calling Lauren's dead husband her 'ex.' Doesn't *'ex'* mean former? If you die, aren't you kind of former? Help me out here. Like I said, I think I made a number of blunders at dinner the other night."

"Maybe to a guy's way of thinking. I'd watch that one if I were you. You need to try and be sensitive to her loss. From what I've heard, Kendall was a great guy. When someone dies, people tend to make them saints anyway, and if they go down in the line of fire . . ."

"Yeah, I get that. I'll never hold a candle to her memory of him as the perfect husband and father. It's just that after having a marriage go south, I'd really like . . ." He swallowed, trying to get his emotions in check. "I'd like to be loved like that someday, too."

Chapter Three

Cut to the Chase

Bryan Everett settled into his favorite recliner and clicked the remote control, pulling up a recorded episode of his favorite show. Over the familiar "da dum" of *Law and Order*, he heard his cell phone playing the theme from *The Pink Panther*, the ringtone he had assigned to his older sister, Samantha. Sami loved anything pink. She was a girly girl, a sales representative for Tara Leigh Cosmetics. Sami was close to achieving a perk-laden cruise trip to Hawaii awarded to the company's highest achievers—the Tara Leigh Cruise, and even her brother the police sergeant was not safe from her sales pitches.

He paused his show and picked up his cell phone. "Hey, Sami. Whaddya need?"

"Don't say it like that, like I only call you when I need something."

"I just thought I'd cut to the chase."

She hesitated. "Okay, so I need something."

"Fire when ready."

"Cut to the chase. Fire when ready. You just can't leave the cop stuff at the precinct, can you?"

"Guilty as charged."

"See, there you go again," she said.

He laughed. "No, that's the legal side. You know, *Law and Order*, the show I was watching before I was so rudely interrupted." He deepened his voice. "In the criminal justice system, the people are represented by two separate yet equally important groups: the police, who investigate crime, and the district attorneys, who prosecute the offenders." He paused for the last dramatic line. "These are their stories."

"Oh, good grief! You've got to get out more."

"So, what is it? Are your sales down? Are you still trying to turn me into a Metrosexual?"

"Oh Bryan, that is *so* 2003."

He rolled his eyes, even though she was not there to read his body language.

"Did you try the face bar I gave you? If you were to share with your fellow officers how it cleanses and buffs your skin . . ."

"Yeah, the soap. Sis, when men, and not even just macho law enforcement men, use the word *buff,* they're not talking about face washing. I'm sorry if this is a setback in your career, but I'm not going to be the TLC go-to guy for the police department in the greater Denver area. And you know what I think of MLMs."

"It helps fight the signs of aging," Sami added.

"One of the signs of aging is finally being smart enough to know when to back off. I'll tell you what. I'll use up that bar of soap, and if, in ten years or so, I look younger than other guys my age, and they clamor around me wanting to know why my face is as smooth as a baby's butt, I'll share the secret of my youthful complexion."

She sighed. "That wasn't it, anyway, but you can't blame a girl for trying."

"Wasn't *it?*" he asked.

"That wasn't what I wanted. You were the one that brought it up, so I thought I'd give it a try. Remember the offer is still on for the Super Bowl pre-party. I'll bring the refreshments."

This wasn't the first time she'd made the offer, and he imagined it was not likely to be the last unless he made his position a little more clear. Apparently ignoring her request hadn't been enough to get the message across. Why didn't women get that? The guy doesn't call back, he isn't interested. If he asks you out again, he *is* interested. If he proposes, he wants to marry you. If he doesn't propose, he doesn't want to marry you. The guy code. It wasn't that hard to crack.

"Sami, would you show up to one of your parties without any make-up on?"

"You know I wouldn't. What kind of a stupid question is that?"

"Of course not, because you need the respect of the people you work with. And I need the respect of my friends and fellow officers, so no make-up party before the Super Bowl. Ya got that? So what *do* you want?" Bryan asked.

"Mom said she gave you Dad's Santa suit."

"It's that time of year. Yeah, I've got the suit. My inheritance," he said dryly. "I still can't figure out why Dad gave it to me instead of Rick."

"Have you used it yet, tried it on?"

"Last year was too soon, Sami. And I'm not exactly as Santa-shaped as Dad was. I've tried to stay buff, you know, thanks to that soap you gave me. I thought I might stick a pillow in there this year and offer my services collecting for our Toys for Tots drive. Why? Karl want to borrow it? I'm not sure I'm ready to do the family party. That was Dad's thing for the grandkids and I'd feel like a cheap imposter. It would probably be easier for Karl to do it than me."

"Um, no. I mean I'll check with Karl and see if he wants to play Santa for the family party, but I was wondering . . ."

"Yeah? Spit it out."

"Some of us from church have gathered some toys and gifts for a young family from our congregation. She lives near me, so I've been the dropoff, and I told them I knew a guy who could play Santa."

"Oh. A Sub-for-Santa?"

"Well, I guess so. I mean, it isn't because they won't have Christmas otherwise. I think they're okay financially. It's a young widow and her little kids, earlier this year was the first anniversary of his death in the military, and we're just trying to cheer them up and do something nice. Her name is Lauren. She's about your age and has two adorable little boys."

She's matchmaking again. "Isn't there somebody from church with a Santa suit?" he asked.

"We're trying to remain anonymous. Barton Griffiths always plays Santa at the church Christmas party. Even though she hasn't lived here very long, she'd recognize him for sure. He's got this loud nasal voice. Frankly, I think he scares some of the kids and if it was up to me . . ."

15

"You're trying to set me up." It wasn't a question. It was a statement. He knew his sister. Ever since he'd turned thirty, with no serious romantic prospects on the horizon, she'd ramped it up a notch. He'd finally told her to back off, that she was not allowed within five hundred feet of his social life. That restraining order was issued after she'd started lining up blind dates for him with relatives of women to whom she sold makeup. "Did you forget that my social life is a no-fly-zone for you?"

"Calm down, Bryan," she said. "You don't have to shoot me down, although I have no doubt you would. I thought you said Brinley was a really nice girl."

"She was. She was very sweet, but the only thing we had in common was that her aunt had bought a mascara from you."

"Lauren's dating someone. At least that's what I've heard. Charlene Hamilton introduced her to her step-brother, Lloyd, whose wife just up and left him. He got custody of their two little girls. Char says things are moving right along, just like a modern-day *Brady Bunch.*"

Bryan knew that if there was anyone who would be up-to-date on such things, it was Sami. "So you're really not trying to set me up? It's just a service project?"

She sighed. "I just need you to be jolly and deliver some toys. You can put a pillow in to fake the belly, but I've gotta say, Bry, Dad did jolly a whole lot better than you."

"Jolly, sure. I can do jolly. Just because I'm not jolly while I'm breaking up domestic violence or arresting the ho, ho, hos on the corner, doesn't mean I can't pull it off once I've got the suit on."

"Maybe it will be like that Tim Allen movie, *The Santa Clause*, and it comes to you once you put on the suit."

"Yeah, like Frosty, the Snowman's magic hat. Okay, Sami, I'll deliver some toys to your friend, and I'll jolly well be jolly. Let me know when you've got everything together."

"Thanks, Bryan." He heard the tremor in her voice. "I know Dad would be happy."

"Sure." He fought back his emotions. Women could get away with that mushy stuff lots better than men could, even men who exfoliated with soap from Tara Leigh Cosmetics.

Chapter Four

Just Friends

Lauren bent over the tub, ignoring the ringing phone as she bathed her two active little boys. Brett closed his eyes tight and began to whimper quietly, as he knew she was about to rinse the shampoo from his hair. Dirk was still wearing his goggles, and he had been underwater enough times that she figured he had rinsed his own hair. The telephone began to ring again. *Just leave a message, whoever you are.* She stopped pouring water for a moment and counted the rings. *Four, same as a few minutes ago. It's him again. He won't leave a message.*

The calls had started a little over a week ago. It had been over a year-and-a-half since Kendall's death. It had been jarring to have someone call and ask for him this long after he'd been gone. If it had been one of his out-of-town friends, someone who might not have heard about his death, she would have been willing to give an update. There had been many news articles about him in the local papers. In this day of social media, she couldn't imagine someone who knew him would not have heard about his heroic death, somehow or other. She wasn't about to tell some disembodied male voice on the telephone that she now lived alone, with a two-year-old and a four-year-old as bodyguards. She had given the standard answer she used for telemarketers.

"Kendall is not available. May I take a message?"

Usually what followed was a sales pitch for some product or politician, and she always made short work of those. Sometimes she did tell the telemarketers that Kendall was dead, just to embarrass them. But this call had been different.

"I really need to talk to Kendall. Is he there?"

"If you leave a name and number, I'll give him the message."

"No, I'll call back. It's really important. When is he going to be home?"

"Where do you know Kendall from?"

"Why are you asking?"

"Why won't you tell me?"

The man on the phone would never identify himself, and therefore, she had never given him more information. She didn't have Caller ID, and she'd thought about getting it, but if he was halfway smart, he was hiding his tracks, so that probably wouldn't help either. She had told herself that he had never said anything threatening and that he would tire of calling her after a time, that it was probably just some nutcase getting his thrills by making her nervous. She feared it was working.

The responsibility she now bore as the sole parent weighed heavily on her shoulders. No more divide and conquer. No more help at the end of the day. Sometimes she found herself wishing that Kendall had been more like her friend Sara's husband, Bryce, inclined to let his wife do everything related to child rearing and home upkeep, believing that the pay stub he gave her every two weeks was his ticket out of those chores. If Kendall had been like Bryce, carrying on without his help might not have been so difficult. She had conveniently forgotten that due to his military career, she had been a functional single parent much of the time. But when he had been home, he had been a fully-engaged hands-on father.

She turned her attention back to the boys and lifted one dripping boy and then the other out of the tub, wrapped them each in a towel and sent them scurrying off to their room to find their pajamas. There had been a time when Lauren cared about matching tops and bottoms, but now if they had on something that covered them at bedtime, she was more than satisfied. She had told them that mixing Batman and Spiderman only gave them more superpowers. "Booperman" was now the name they gave to any combination of Superhero pajamas.

She stood on the bottom rail of the bunk bed and whispered to her redheaded son on the top bunk. "I love you, Dirk. Daddy loves you, too. We are both so proud of you." She glanced at "Half-Daddy" that Dirk insisted be laid at the end of his bed at night. How could Kendall have known when he had them made that someday that was all they would have left of him? Now that

20

Kendall was away permanently, Dirk was even more attached to his cardboard daddy. The counselor she had been seeing had told her that anything that gave her son comfort was good. She gave cardboard Kendall a quick salute and climbed down and leaned over her sandy-haired little one in the bottom bunk. She had read in a parenting magazine at the doctor's office that the last thing you say to your children at night is repeated in their subconscious mind as they sleep. "Brett, Mom and Dad love you so much. Good night. Sweet dreams."

After she had them settled in, she decided to turn in herself, earlier than usual. Fishing in her middle drawer where she kept her warm pajamas, she came up with the bottoms of one pair and the top of another. *Good enough. I guess tonight I'll be Booperman, too.* Dressed in a pink snowflake top and forest-green polar bear bottoms, she picked up the receiver of the phone by her bed, checking for the stuttering dial tone that would tell her that someone had left a message. The tone was steady, which came as no surprise.

She banned thoughts of the mystery caller from her mind. She had decided that if the last messages of the day repeated for children, the last messages of the day she gave herself should also be positive. The evening news often left her with discouraging and depressing messages, so she had simply stopped watching. She had started collecting biographies of people who had endured difficult things, hoping her mind would latch onto any strategy that might help her face a future without Kendall. Picking up the latest book, she opened to chapter five, reading about actress Teri Garr's battle with multiple sclerosis.

Morning came quickly. Before the boys were up, she pulled her plush maroon bathrobe around her, yet another clashing part of her eclectic outfit, shoving her feet into the warm slippers she kept near the bed. Her home had tile and hardwood floors, neither of which provided a lick of warmth during the winter months. She headed to the kitchen and poured a little cat food into a bowl. For several months she had been trying to lure a skinny gray stray cat into her garage. Lauren had named the cat Gollum, before she had realized the skittish feline had two kittens. Still, she kept the name. It fit. And Gollum's gender wasn't exactly clear from the movie anyway she had told herself. She opened the garage door, placing the bowl of food just inside. She'd seen the mother cat face down a dog several times her size in defense of her babies, and ever since then, Lauren had seen the feisty mother cat as a kindred spirit.

As winter had approached, Lauren had bought a warm cat bed that she kept in the garage. She set the bowl of food next to the bowl of milk she had poured, both inside the bed so the cat would have to get inside it to eat and would discover how warm and cozy it was. "Here Gollum. Here kitty kitty." She saw that the cat and her half-grown kittens were curled up under her car in the driveway. Although the kittens were no longer tiny, they stayed close to their mother and skittered away any time Lauren approached them.

Her automatic garage door opener was broken, and most of the time it just seemed easier to hurry the kids into the house through the front door than to bother with manually opening the garage door. It was on her to-do-list to get it fixed.

"You can bring your babies in and keep them warm. It's tough being a single mom, isn't it? I suppose it's about time I gave them names, too. How about if we call them Bilbo and Frodo?" Gollum eyed the food hungrily, but Lauren knew that the cat would not come near it until the human was gone.

Lauren trudged through the snow to retrieve the morning paper from the end of the driveway, her head down to avoid the light flakes of snow still falling, giving the cat a chance to dart into the garage with her hungry offspring right behind her.

As Lauren reached down to pick up the end of the plastic bag protecting her paper, a pair of brown hiking boots came into view. She jerked upward and found herself staring into the smiling face of Lloyd Owens.

She pulled her bathrobe shut, cinching the belt. "L – Lloyd," she stuttered.

"Actually, the second L is silent," he smiled.

"Not when you ambush me in my driveway at seven in the morning. What are you doing here?"

"We're staying with Charlene for the holidays. From her kitchen, I can look up the hill from the next street down and see when your garage door goes up. I was just sitting there having a bowl of Fruit Loops and I saw it open and worried something might be the matter, so I came over."

She contemplated whether the better choice was to stand shivering out in the driveway in her pajamas or to invite him into the house. This was not Lloyd's first pop-in visit since their disastrous date. Although she had sidestepped further invitations from him so far, she knew she needed to be clear with him once and for all that she simply wasn't interested. But he had a way of looking hopeful and excited about the possibility of spending more time together, and so she had given him excuses rather than the truth. She settled on inviting him into the garage, although out of the corner of her eye she could see the cat and kittens hungrily devouring the kibbles and knew they would take flight as she approached. Nevertheless, she motioned Lloyd into the garage, hoping to clear things up with him and bring her feline friends back shortly.

"Lloyd, we went out to dinner once." *As a favor to your sister, because she is my friend.* "You, um, have gone over and above the call of duty in checking in on us these last couple of weeks, but we're fine. Frankly, it's a little disconcerting, the thought of you sitting there staring at my house." *And I might delay getting the automatic opener fixed now that I know that you're sitting in your sister's kitchen fixating on my garage door every morning.*

"It was so early in the morning, I thought something might be wrong with one of the boys."

"No, everybody is fine. We're fine." She was torn between feeling grateful that someone was looking out for her and annoyed that this man she barely knew had appointed himself her guardian. In the final analysis, her gratitude was eclipsed by his behavior that bordered on stalking. She swallowed. "I really don't need you checking in on us." He still wasn't getting it.

"I had such a good time when we went out to dinner. I don't think it's a coincidence that we're a family in search of a mother and you and your boys are a family in search of a father. I just had

23

such good feelings that we could be a workable solution for each other."

Boy, this guy moves fast. Workable? Is that all he wants, workable? "That's just it, Lloyd. We *aren't* a family in search of a father. We're a family grieving the loss of a husband and father. I'm afraid the only confirmation I had from our dinner the other night was a realization that it is too soon for me to date. I thought I made that clear when you brought me home. I apologize if you would like things to be otherwise. I should have listened to my instincts and told Charlene that when she offered to set us up and it would have made things easier for both of us."

"But hasn't it been well over a year since your husband died? Even in the olden days, I think widows stopped wearing black after a year."

"Lloyd, that first year I was completely in survival mode, trying to straighten out our finances, figuring out what we had and didn't have, collecting insurance, making more financial decisions, having to relocate quickly with two little ones in tow. That this house came on the market at the right time and at the right price was a big blessing in my life, but when I moved, I lost a support system of other wives who understood."

"Fort Collins isn't that far away," he said.

"I've tried to keep in touch, but now I feel I'm just a reminder of what could happen to them. It isn't the same. I can feel those friendships falling away."

"That must be hard."

"It is. And you have no idea all the decisions I've had to make, all the while trying to shove out of my mind images of what happened to my husband. I finally have the feeling that I'm getting some sort of routine and normalcy for myself and my children. No matter what anybody else thinks of the timing, it's *my* choice to decide when to add romantic complications to my life. When I do, I'll probably start interviewing babysitters and reviewing their references. Who can say how long that process will take?"

"There are new friends to be made." He blew on his hands. "It's cold. Why don't we go inside and talk?"

24

She stood her ground. "I've already said more than I mean to, more than I should have. I'm not dressed. I haven't had a shower. I haven't even combed my hair." She ran her hand through her unkempt hair. "The boys are still asleep. I certainly wasn't expecting company."

"I think you look beautiful."

She spoke slowly. "I am going inside. You need to go back over to your sister's house." At the stricken look on his face, she added kindly, "Your Fruit Loops are probably all soggy by now. And your daughters . . ."

"They're still asleep." He frowned. "You're not even going to invite me in?"

She shook her head. "Nope, I'm not. Lloyd, you can't just pop in on me like this. At least you need to call first."

"Okay Lauren, I get that you aren't ready to date, yet, but can't we still be supportive as friends, as a couple of single parents struggling? Why do you think I spend so much time at my sister's house, anyway? I know how lonely and quiet it gets in the evenings. I apologize if I've been intrusive, but I don't know how to be both Mom and Dad. I figured when I met you, I had found someone who sort of understood about that, from the other direction. If you've lost your support system, don't you need to rebuild a new one?"

Lauren softened somewhat. "Okay, sure, friends. But right now, I really do need to get inside and get warm. And you need to go."

Chapter Five

Spilled Milk

L auren had dropped Dirk off at his preschool and was looking forward to a quiet afternoon. With any luck, Brett would go down for a nap, and she'd be able to catch up on some lost sleep as well. She didn't know why it was easier for her to fall asleep in the light of day than at night, but she'd come to count on her afternoon naps on preschool days to get her through the week.

The Christmas tree was up thanks to help from Luke, one of Kendall's best friends from high school. He had stayed in the area and they had socialized with him and his wife from time to time, when Kendall was around. It was a blessing also to have Luke in their church congregation, someone that they would see every Sunday with whom they were already friends and who had known Kendall.

Luke checked in with them every Sunday, not by asking Lauren what she needed or how she was doing but by asking Dirk. That was how he had heard of the Christmas tree leaning up against the wall because Mom couldn't get it into the stand by herself. So the tree was now up and she knew she needed to get it decorated before Dirk ratted her off about that, too. Still, that day she walked past the three boxes of ornaments, lights, and tinsel near the base of the tree, successfully ignoring them as she'd done for the past week. Next to the tree stood the half-size cardboard cutout of Kendall.

In addition to Luke and Melissa and their children, Lauren had made an effort to befriend a few other people from church whose homes were near hers, in an effort to rebuild her support system and have people close by that she could call on in an emergency. Now that Lloyd was fixating on her garage door from his sister's kitchen, she wasn't sure if it had been such a good idea. Close friends would be there for you, but they also tended to feel they had meddling rights beyond those of mere acquaintances.

She'd been invited to a couple of make-up parties Samantha Bridges had thrown, who also lived nearby, and had even run into a girl who used to date Kendall at one of the parties. Heidi Markham was still single, and Lauren hadn't been sure how to proceed, because she hadn't exactly picked up on a friendly or sympathetic vibe from Kendall's old flame. She didn't remember him ever mentioning Heidi. He'd mentioned dating a number of different girls in high school, but Heidi had been quite willing to talk at length of her time spent with Kendall, as if she had been trying to one-up his young widow and show she still had claim to a small corner of his heart. While she was interested in befriending people with fond memories of her dear departed husband, Lauren had left Heidi off the list of potential new friends.

Lauren wasn't sure how long she'd been asleep when she was startled awake by the ringing phone next to the bed. She scrambled for the phone, knocking over the half-full glass of milk she'd left on the nightstand. "Hello." She grabbed the bath towel she'd left on the bed after her morning shower, mopping up milk from the floor and nightstand as she talked.

"Lauren, it's Mom."

"Oh hi, Mom. Just mopping up a little spilled milk here, so I'm going to put you on speaker."

"Well, you know what they say . . ."

"Sure. As if I don't have better things to cry about than spilled milk. So how are you?"

"We're fine." She paused. "Dad's about to book the tickets, and I just wanted to make sure you're going to be okay during the holidays alone if we take this trip."

"We survived last year, and we'll survive this year. Mom, you're well past the age where you deny yourself a trip because of your children. Your husband is taking you to Italy. It's your 35th wedding anniversary. Go already." She threw the towel down on

28

the floor and stepped on it, soaking up the milk from the area rug near the bed.

"I can't stand the thought of the three of you there alone."

"We'll be fine." She didn't mention the benefit of having Kendall's family nearby because the two mothers had not exactly been fast friends since playing dueling Grandmas when they had both showed up to help Lauren with her first baby. "We're going to have a very low-key Christmas. I'll buy the boys some toys, and they'll play with them. You missed your 25th anniversary trip because of Dad's appendicitis. Now go. You deserve this trip."

"How is Dirk? Is he still . . .?"

"He went to preschool without it today. I've been following the counselor's advice and finding reasons to leave our cardboard dad home to watch over things. Today he's guarding our Christmas tree and the presents under it from the Grinch."

"And Brett. Is he still not talking? He's almost three."

"Mom, he didn't *stop* talking. He just never started."

"Either way, I worry about him."

"He's fine, Mom. He's fine. He understands everything I say. It's in there. He says 'hungry' and 'mama.' So far that's getting him by. You had four kids. Did we all do everything on the same time schedule?"

Her mother knew when to stop. "I'm glad to hear you've got a tree up. That's good!"

"Yeah, it's up." *Not decorated but it's up.* "There are lots of presents under it. People have been very generous, almost as much as last year. I guess the thought of two little boys without a father at Christmas still touches people's hearts." She lifted the reading lamp and mopped up the milk at its base.

"I can only imagine what people thought when you propped him up in a pew at his own funeral."

Are we back to that again? "Mother, I'm beyond caring what anyone thinks of anything I do. Dirk was very upset about leaving him in the car. At the time, I thought it would have been far worse to have him making a scene about it. Tom Sawyer attended his own funeral, so why couldn't Kendall? Besides, there was the cardboard cutout of him in his camouflage standing by the casket,

29

so what was wrong with there being another one there in the pew with his son?" She tried to crowd out thoughts that no one seemed to understand, about how a conversation about her cardboard husband standing by his closed coffin conjured up thoughts of the events that had necessitated a closed coffin, of the IED explosion that had ended her husband's life.

She forced herself back to the conversation. "As I look back, I actually think it was kind of funny." Lauren knew her straight-laced mother had been mortified by what was surely a breach of etiquette, if anyone had thought to make rules regarding such things. Personally, Lauren felt that if people couldn't understand the fragile feelings of two little boys and forgive anything out of the ordinary they might do or say at the time of their father's death, it was their problem, not hers.

"It was jarring, Lauren. That's what it was, to see a replica of him sitting there at his own funeral."

"I went to a funeral once for a fellow who had an identical twin brother who lived in another state. His friends all knew he was a twin, but I guess a lot of his co-workers didn't know he had a twin, much less one that looked just like him. His brother talked at the funeral. There were a few gasps when he walked up to the pulpit. He said something like, 'I hope I didn't scare any of you.' I remember thinking how strange that would be for his wife, to have this brother-in-law who looked just like her husband around for the rest of her life. So yeah, sometimes when Brett has moved one of the cardboard dads somewhere, it takes me by surprise, too, but I'm pretty much used to having a two-dimensional husband by now. I've got camouflage Kendall upstairs in my bedroom."

"Good grief, Lauren. Tell me you don't *sleep* with it!"

"Give me some credit, Mother. No, I have him stand by the window so it looks like there's a man in the house."

"All that is likely to accomplish is to get your neighbors to gossip about you."

"That's what I'm going for, so they'll stop lining me up with bad blind dates." She paused, wishing she could take those last words back. She continued on, hoping to distract her mother. "Actually, you can only see that one from the backyard."

Her mother pounced. "*What?* You've been on a *date?*"

Lauren sighed. She hadn't planned on telling her mother about her date with Lloyd.

"Tell me about it. What's his name? What is he like?"

"His name is Lloyd Owens. Sounds like someone *you* should be dating, doesn't it? I go to church with his sister who lives in the next block down, so we've gotten to know each other reasonably well, riding together to a couple of church parties. She set us up. He's recently divorced, and he has two little girls."

"Isn't that perfect?"

"Mom, you know this isn't like matching up socks, don't you?"

"Dads don't often get custody. That must speak well of him. Did you have a good time?"

"No, not really. I felt like I was cheating on Kendall, and . . ."

"Now don't miss out on a live prospect just because you aren't ready."

"Mother, you need to go to Italy and stop worrying about me."

"Are you going to go out with him again?"

"I don't think so. I've already told him I'm not ready to date." She tossed the soggy towel into the hamper. "Mom, I really should go and do a better job of cleaning up so my bedroom doesn't smell like sour milk tomorrow."

"Promise me one thing, honey. Promise me you'll give this Lloyd fellow a chance."

Lauren sighed. "Okay, if that's what it takes for you to have a good time on vacation without worrying about me, I'll give him a chance."

Chapter Six

Pulling Santa's Beard

S amantha surveyed her brother. "You're right. Dad made a much better Santa than you do. Let's lose the pillow. It looks like a . . ."

"Like a pillow?" he asked.

"Exactly! Here." She opened her closet and rummaged around in a sewing basket. "Let's try some of this batting. Then we can put in as much as we want and make you look naturally more pudgy. You're probably the thinnest of all the family Santas so far, unless great great-grandfather Isaac was a skinny Depression-era Santa." She chatted on while she stuffed her brother's midsection. "I called Lauren a few minutes ago to talk about her food assignment for the Christmas pot-luck, so I know she's home. She was kind of short with me at first because apparently she'd just had a disturbing call of some sort and I called right afterwards. She didn't explain much about it, but she thought I was him calling again. If you go over now, you've still got some light left."

After a few minutes Sami stood back and surveyed her handiwork. "That's much better. And it was a good call to get a new beard."

"It wasn't cheap. That's my contribution to your little service project. Dad's Santa beard needed an upgrade. Any kid worth his salt always pulls Santa's beard."

"Really? I never did."

"I *always* did. If it was a really cheap one that looped over his ears, you could pull it way down and let it flap back in his face."

"No wonder I always got more for Christmas than you did."

Bryan hoisted the big bag of gifts and toys onto the backseat in his extended-cab black pick-up truck and followed the directions his sister had given him. He soon pulled up in front of the Baylor house. It was just starting to get dark, and there were lights on in the house. He rang the doorbell and hoped he would do his father proud with his first attempt at imitating Father Christmas.

The door opened. In the doorway stood a woman about his age in a red sweater and jeans, her blondish-brown hair pulled into a loose ponytail. Even dressed down and without her hair done and wearing minimal makeup, or maybe because of those things, he found her attractive, but he reminded himself that wasn't why he was there. Behind her a little boy with red hair peeked at him, eyes wide.

She narrowed her eyes and looked at him as she spoke, the tone of her voice cheerful despite the suspicious look in her eyes. "Brett, come here! It's Santa Claus at our house and it isn't even Christmas yet!" Soon another little boy with hair like his mother was staring wordlessly up at Bryan expectantly.

So far so good. "Ho ho ho! Merry Christmas!" He set down his pack, a green burlap bag that had also been part of his father's Santa shtick, although it had seen better days and would likely need replacing before long. He waited for her to open the screen door and invite him in. "My elves and I have been busy at the North Pole and we've got a bag full of gifts for you.

Lauren had been smiling, at least the bottom half of her face had been, but suddenly her smile disappeared and she eyed the bag suspiciously. "Let Santa in, Mommy!" Dirk pleaded. "He's got toys!" Bryan had a vague recollection of his younger days when toys were one of the main reasons for living. Dirk started to open the door, but his mother was way ahead of him and wedged her foot in front of the screen door.

Lauren smiled again, but this one seemed forced. "So Santa," she said pointedly. "Do I *know* you?"

Perplexed, he answered. "Yeah, I'm Santa." *What else am I supposed to say with your two little kids staring up at me?*

"I'm sorry, but I don't recognize you or your voice," she said. "Maybe if you can tell me the names of your elves . . ."

"My elves? How about I list off my reindeer? There's Dasher and Dancer and . . ."

"Woodolph," said little Brett seriously, bringing his list of vocabulary words to three.

34

Lauren took a moment to react. She kneeled down and embraced her youngest son. "That's right, Brett! Rudolph is Santa's reindeer with the big red nose."

She stood up again, staring hard at Bryan. He stared right back into the depths of her expressive green eyes, eyes that showed an immeasurable sadness. Right then and there he knew he wanted to be the one to make those eyes look happy again someday. If he was reading her right, he could see that she was conflicted. If he had been able to read her thoughts, he might have understood that she wanted to be able to trust her gut instinct and what she saw in his eyes, that a part of her wanted to let him in.

"My elves," he tried again. "Lauren, my elves worked very hard to make these toys and they wanted to give them to you without any thanks. It really wouldn't be right for me to tell you the names of the particular elves, especially the bossy head elf. She'd be really mad at me if I let the cat out of the bag."

"Santa brought me a kitty?" Brett asked.

Bryan stifled a chuckle, reminding himself that around little kids you have to choose your words carefully. "If I could tell you who she is, you'd understand."

She smiled a little at that. "Okay, you know *my* name, Santa. If you come on behalf of someone who knows me, what are the names of my boys?"

Oh, dang! Samantha told me.

"Um, unusual names, I remember. You know, Santa has to remember all the names of all the kids in the world so . . ." Dirk looked like he was about to cry. "Is it Derek and Brad?"

"I'm sorry, Santa, but unless you can tell me some good reason I should trust you . . ." He heard footsteps behind him. He didn't know who it was coming up the walk, but there was no mistaking the look of gratitude in her eyes.

Bryan had no way of knowing that she was caught between the possibility that he was legitimately there on behalf of friends and the possibility that he might actually be her mysterious caller or associated with him somehow, so she erred on the side of safety, elevating Lloyd to a new status. "Santa, this is my *boyfriend*, Lloyd. Lloyd, *Santa* stopped by, but I'm not sure I know him, so he was just leaving and . . ." Bryan's heart plunged. His first foray as St. Nick was not going well, but beyond that, this beautiful woman was already involved with someone. He could have kicked himself for taking such a hard line with Sami on blind dates.

Lloyd suddenly puffed out his chest, doing his best to look taller than he was, especially next to this Santa who had a good four inches on him. "Santa, you heard the lady. Get lost!" She opened the door that had been shut to him and Lloyd happily went inside.

Bryan exchanged one last quick look with Lauren through the screen door, reading something like regret mixed with fear in her expression. It was obvious that fear had won out. He picked up the bag and muttered one last feeble "ho ho ho" and hoisted it onto his back. He turned to wave to the little boys, hoping they had not been scarred too much by this cryptic visit from the jolly old elf. What he saw instead was Lauren kissing Lloyd.

This must have been the guy Sami had mentioned, someone's brother. They appeared to be almost the same height. He supposed that worked okay for kissing. He'd dated a few short girls and goodnight kisses at the door had sometimes been awkward, first kisses especially. There was too much time on approach, that was it, too much time to wonder if you'd read the signals right. As the kiss ended, he got a quick look at her face and was puzzled at what he saw. The look on her face didn't add up, not if they were boyfriend and girlfriend.

He was a police officer, trained to interpret the micro-emotions expressed on people's faces—a fleeting look of recognition, averted eyes that bespoke guilt, or the look on the face of a woman when she hadn't wanted to be kissed. He had been single long enough to recognize that look. What he'd seen had not been Lauren kissing Lloyd. It had been Lloyd kissing Lauren.

Bryan tossed his Santa bag into the back of the truck, not worrying about whether or not it was going to get wet from the standing snow in the bed of the truck, muttering to himself. "Well, did you see that, Dad? My first gig as Santa. I'm a natural, huh? At this rate, I'm bound to be the last of the family Santas. She did everything but pull on my beard and let it flap back in my face."

Then he hit himself in the forehead with the heel of his hand. *Tara Leigh! Why didn't I mention there was probably a TLC lipstick in the bag? She would have known it was Samantha and I would have been in the clear for technically not giving anything away.*

It might have been his imagination, but he could have sworn he could almost hear his father laughing.

Chapter Seven

A Kiss Is Still a Kiss

As Santa's black truck pulled away, Lauren angrily pulled away from Lloyd, who had wrapped his arms tightly around her, his nose in her hair, drinking in the scent of her vanilla shampoo.

"What was *that?*"

"Wow, it *has* been a long time, if you don't remember." Lloyd smiled.

"And in front of my boys? The only reason I didn't slap your face is because I don't think my boys needed any further trauma tonight, after watching me shake down Santa."

"You *said* I was your boyfriend. I was just trying to make it look authentic, for Santa."

Lauren narrowed her eyes. "Oh, you didn't do that for *Santa,* Lloyd."

"I was in the moment. Oh come on, you've got to admit it felt good. Was it as good for you as it was for me?"

At his question, Lauren realized she had felt nothing. The kiss had been unwelcome, but in the movies they often showed kisses where the woman started by resisting and ended by willingly participating. But for Lauren, the needle had not moved. Frosty had not begun to melt in the slightest. Before she could answer, armed and ready to tell him just how unwelcome and intrusive his kiss and embrace had been, an angry four-year-old kicked him soundly in the shin.

"Hey, what was *that* for?" Lloyd asked.

"You made Santa go away! He had toys! And a cat!" Dirk started to cry. "He made Santa go away, and now we aren't going to get any presents. And Santa Claus didn't even know our names! Didn't he get my letter you helped me write, Mom?" he asked, between sobs. Brett looked on soberly and Lauren could only guess at what was going on in his little head. There had been so many emotions swirling around them over the past year or so, who knew what he comprehended and what he didn't?

Lloyd watched Lauren kneel down and minister to the pain of her little boy. "Of course Santa got your letter. That's probably why he came by today. Like Santa said, he has to remember the names of lots and lots of kids. He was close when he tried to remember your name." As she said that, she felt a flood of sympathetic feelings for the unknown Santa wash over her, again.

What's wrong with me? I did the right thing. She couldn't forget those eyes. They were all she'd had to take measure of him—as a man, as a person. She realized she had come very close to letting the strange Santa in, based on her feelings, but the overprotective mother in her had won out. Lauren had always been one to trust her gut reaction to people, but common sense had to triumph over pure emotion. She imagined a crime scene after Santa had taken everything of value from her home.

"Why on earth did you let him in, Ma'am?"

"Well officer, he had nice eyes."

She came back to the present. "He came to our house and that means he knows who you are and where we live so he can come back on Christmas Eve."

"Hey, the kid kicked me. Aren't you going to do a timeout or something?" Lloyd asked.

All of her contempt for Lloyd came out in two words. "The *kid*?"

"Calm down, Lauren. I know his name. I'm not like Santa."

Don't remind him. She turned to her oldest son. "Dirk, why don't you get two presents from under the tree and you and Brett can open them early. Get those two in the green snowman paper."

She headed into the family room with Lloyd right behind her and watched her two little boys start tearing into the wrapping, soon happily playing with two plastic characters from the last *Toy Story* movie.

"You're letting them open presents three weeks before Christmas? Do you want your children growing up with some kind of entitlement mentality or what? It's like you're rewarding him for kicking me."

40

She plopped down on the sectional sofa, making sure there were a couple of throw pillows next to her so that Lloyd would keep his distance when he sat down.

"Give me a break, Lloyd. If they have a new toy to play with, maybe they'll forget the trauma of this whole afternoon and they won't be listening in on our conversation about why I wouldn't let Santa in."

He noticed the pillow trick, something she'd tried before on him, and sat down on the far end of the sofa. "You don't have to set up the defensive pillows, Lauren. I'll stay on my side of the sofa. So that boyfriend thing was just for Santa's benefit, huh? I thought I'd had a promotion or something."

She let that comment go by without a response.

"Who was that anyway?" he asked.

"If I knew, I wouldn't have been giving him the third degree. Some guy in a Santa suit shows up on my porch. He could be anyone. Who knows what could be in the bag. I'm not going to let him in."

"Good call on keeping Santa at bay, but you could let down some of your defenses around *me*, you know. If he comes back, I'm just a phone call away."

At the mention of that, Lauren remembered the phone call from earlier in the day. "I had another call from that guy, the one who won't leave his name."

"What did he say this time?"

"Same as always, except for at the end. He asked for Kendall. I told him he wasn't here, asked if I could take a message. He said there wasn't any message. Then he said he doubted I could get a message to him and hung up."

Lloyd moved a couple of feet closer. "That must be so disturbing. Don't you have Caller ID or something?"

"No. I tried to do that call-return thing but it didn't work. The recording said the call could not be returned. I figure whoever is doing this is covering their tracks and Caller ID would probably end up being an unnecessary expense that doesn't accomplish anything either. I actually thought about cancelling my landline completely, but there's security in a landline. It is always there. It doesn't need charging, doesn't get lost, doesn't fall out of your purse in the garage and get run over. So anyway, that really didn't seem like a good idea. I've taught Dirk how to call 9-1-1 on the phone in an emergency."

He scooted a little bit closer, up to the pillow barrier. "That's got to be so scary for you. Have you thought about getting an unlisted number?"

"That's kind of drastic. Besides, you give it out to a couple of friends and neighbors and soon it's on the church list and then before you know it, somehow every telemarketer from here to Chicago has it. I've just successfully taught Dirk our address and phone number. Besides that, I don't know. It's like letting a terrorist win."

"Do you think that strange Santa might have been your mystery caller?"

She nodded her head. "It crossed my mind that it could have been him. I like to think I would recognize the voice, but the guy on the phone speaks in kind of hushed tones, so I'm not sure what his voice would sound like normally. I don't know what to think. In rational moments I tell myself it's just some jerk who read the articles about Kendall and is getting some kind of perverse enjoyment out of prank calling to scare me. Other times I imagine he knows where I live, might do something to one of my boys."

Lloyd picked up one of the pillows and moved it out of the way. He was close enough that he reached over and put his hand on her arm. "I know I probably blew it today, but I'm here for you, Lauren. I want you to feel protected."

She looked over at him. He seemed sincerely worried about her. She so wanted to feel safe and protected again. Maybe her mother was right that she should give Lloyd a chance. This time she didn't resist when he moved closer and put his arm on her shoulder in a protective gesture. He glanced up, and Lauren noticed his scowl as he saw a life-size cardboard cutout of Kendall across the room that seemed to be staring right at him. "How many of those things do you have?"

"What?"

"Your cardboard bodyguards. Do they move around on their own or do you rearrange them, like moving the furniture?"

"Counting the half-size one that rides in the car, we've got four. That's the one that Dirk is most attached to. Then we've got this one in his dress uniform, one in his civvies, and there's another in camouflage." *That I keep in my bedroom. And that you'll likely never meet.* "Kendall had them made for the boys before his last deployment. And I moved that one to make room for the Christmas tree." She neglected to mention that yes, she had deliberately placed him across from the sofa they usually sat on when Lloyd popped by for one of his unannounced visits.

"How long do you plan on keeping them?"

"I don't have any plans for *not* keeping them. What do you think I'm going to do, wake up one morning and throw Dad away?"

"I know you said you've talked to your counselor about Dirk and his attachment to the cardboard dads, but I'm wondering if you've talked about *your* attachment to them. Of course, you can continue to hide behind your children and . . ."

She fixed him with a cold stare, pulling away from the arm on her shoulder. "How exactly do you think this is any of your business? Okay, I'll admit it. It isn't just the boys. You hear about people who go talk to their loved ones and sit at the cemetery? Yeah, you know what, Lloyd? Sometimes I sit here on this sofa and I talk to my cardboard husband. I talk to him about the boys, about my life, about whatever's on my mind. And it helps me not feel so alone. So put me in the loony bin! I don't think you get it. I don't think you *can* get it. Your situation is too different from mine. You don't understand. You just don't understand."

"I just don't see how you're ever going to move on. I mean, when he was alive he could only be in one room at a time, but he's here staring at me from almost every room in your house."

She picked up a beige throw pillow and hugged it to her chest and smiled. "I know. It works even better than the pillows, doesn't it?"

Chapter Eight

Santa's Employee Review

Samantha heard Bryan slam the door to his truck. She gave a quick stir to the spaghetti noodles in the pot and hurried out into the driveway.

"That was fast. So was she surprised? How did it go?"

Bryan gestured to the back of the truck where the bag of gifts still sat. He retrieved the bag, shaking off the snow, and followed her into the house, plopping the soggy sack down in the corner of the laundry room. He pulled out a chair and sat down at the dinner table, eyeing the chocolate chip cookies cooling on a rack nearby.

He scowled. "Just give me the cookies and milk and nobody gets hurt."

"Oh Bryan, don't go all Sad Sack on me. What happened? Wasn't she home? Why are you in such a curmudgeonly mood? Why don't you have a late dinner with us and then try again later?"

"No, she was home. She wouldn't let me in. You know how you didn't want to send over the guy from church because she'd recognize him? Well, she wouldn't let me in because she *didn't* recognize me. I told her some friends sent me, but you didn't want me to blow your cover so . . . ."

"It's my fault. I should have thought of that. Of course she would be suspicious. I'd probably do the same thing if I was a single mom with a couple of little kids at home."

"It isn't like I could pull out my Santa resumé or something."

"You could have told her you came from a long and distinguished line of Santas. Dad and all his freebies. I wonder if he felt like a disappointment to Grandad. Grandma said he was very successful during the holidays as a department store Santa, made enough money to pay for Christmas and then some."

"Dad sure never did. He never made any money and probably gave away half of what was supposed to be for us to kids who needed the stuff more."

"Do you know if anybody has a photo of our great grandfather or great great-grandfather as Santa? I've heard all the stories about the Santa suit his wife sewed for him during the Depression."

"I've never seen any. It would be interesting to see what a homemade Santa suit looked like," she said. "But you're right, your Santa pedigree wouldn't have scored you any points with Lauren."

"I was actually impressed that she didn't just open the door and usher me in. I wanted to convince her she could trust me, but I didn't have any ammunition. But I've got to ask you, Sami, if there was a beautiful single woman like that in your circle of friends, why *didn't* you introduce me to her? She's even tall."

"For starters, I haven't known her very long, and she still seemed to be in survival mode. The timing just didn't seem right. I've actually thought about it, but you've told me to butt out."

He couldn't exactly contest that. "It figures I would shoot myself in the foot."

"I thought you shot yourself in the shin."

"Very funny! They tested the gun. It had a hair trigger."

"Come on. Stay to dinner anyway. I'm just waiting for the spaghetti to cook and it's probably about ready now. The sauce is already done. It'll just be the three of us tonight. The kids have a school thing, so we're having a late dinner." She pulled a noodle out of the pan and bit into it, turning off the burner. "Also I didn't introduce you because I wasn't sure she was ready to date yet."

"If she isn't ready to date, how come someone else set her up with her brother? That must have been him," Bryan said.

"Who?"

"Oh, a guy came along just as I was getting ready to leave. She introduced him as her boyfriend, but . . ."

"Did she tell you his name?" Samantha dumped the spaghetti into a colander and rinsed it under the faucet.

"Lloyd. Who names their kid Lloyd anymore, anyway?"

"Yeah, that's him," she said.

"I'm not buying it. Something didn't fit."

"Yes, *detective?*"

"I'm a sergeant, not a detective, but you think all law enforcement terms are interchangeable, so whatever. Yeah, I've got some detective skills. Besides that I'm thirty-one and single. That means I've been through a fair number of relationships. I know what a woman looks like after you kiss her, I mean when she enjoyed it. He grabbed her and kissed her, but I think it was for my benefit. I caught a look at her face as they came apart, as much as he would let her anyway. It looked more like he had her in a death grip than a romantic embrace. She didn't look like a woman who wanted to be kissed. Remember in high school when Jennifer Lorenzo was hanging around me all the time, trying to get to my best friend. I thought it was me she liked and I went in for the kill one time."

"Honestly, Bryan. Do you ever listen to yourself? 'Out of ammunition.' 'Death grip.' 'Going in for the kill.'"

"Occupational hazard. Sorry. So anyway, I kissed Jennifer one night after we'd been hanging out together. I thought it was great, but she had this look on her face afterwards that told me loud and clear the kiss had been unwelcome. Being the straight-forward kind of guy I am, I asked her about it. We'd become good enough friends by then that she confessed she was hanging around me to get to Mike. Anyway, that's ancient history, and Mike never did ask her out, but your friend Lauren, as I turned to wave to the little boys, in hopes of salvaging some Christmas spirit, I saw that same look on her face."

"Don't ask *me*. I've been married too long. I'd probably say something like bad breath."

"Yeah, that's probably it. She's madly in love with him, but he didn't hold the onions on his Big Mac."

"Whatever it is, it's between them. I'm sorry I didn't introduce you to her so you could have gotten there first, but if you recall, the first thing you did when I mentioned her name was accuse me of matchmaking, so it's your own fault, Bryan. Anyway, don't get all mopey on me, not at Christmas." She carried a couple of plates to the table. "Karl should be home any minute. You'll probably feel better if you get out of the suit."

"Ya think?"

47

"I think you left your clothes in Mark's room. You can go change in there." She reached into a nearby cupboard. "Here's a garbage bag to put the stuffing in. Try not to make a mess with it. I've already vacuumed in there today."

Sami dished up a plate of spaghetti for her brother and handed it to him when he came out of the bedroom. "Karl came home while you were changing, so we started without you." He pulled out a chair and set his plate down at the table, sitting across from his brother-in-law.

"Sorry to hear your first stint as Santa didn't go well," Karl said.

"I hung the suit in Mark's closet. Sami said you might want to wear it for the family party. I wasn't in it too long, didn't sweat in it much until your friend Lauren patted me down for weapons."

Karl laughed. "She's holding it together under some pretty rough circumstances. Her little boys are all she has left. I don't blame her for being a little over protective. If you want to come to our church Christmas party this Saturday, I'll see that you get a proper introduction."

Normally Bryan would have seen this as a transparent effort to get him out to church services more often, even just to a church party, but the idea of meeting Lauren overcame his reluctance to be shepherded by his faithful churchgoing sister and her husband. "That sounds fun, actually."

Samantha did not hide her surprise. "Really? You'll go?"

"If she meets you out of the suit, realizes you're okay, maybe you can still deliver the toys," Karl added.

Samantha jumped in. "But we didn't want her to know they were from us."

"How much Tara Leigh stuff did you put in there for her, Sam? She's going to know you were part of it. From there, she'll know it was her church friends."

"I just thought she could use some new makeup. She's been looking kind of tired lately."

Bryan immediately jumped to her defense. "I thought she looked beautiful just the way she was. Her husband died serving

48

his country. She's got two little kids to run after. Of course she's tired!"

Karl turned to look at his brother-in-law, surprised at the vigor with which he jumped to Lauren's defense. Bryan suddenly became very interested in his spaghetti. "So I hope you put some bubble bath and stress-relief stuff in there, too."

"I did," Samantha said. "I put a bunch of aromatherapy in for her. We've got three new scents, and there's lots of great stuff in her stocking."

Bryan could feel that Karl was still looking at him, even as Samantha was off on another Tara Leigh sales pitch. "Did Sam tell you about her husband? I've never lost anyone closer than a grandparent, but I can only imagine that some things take longer to get over than others."

"Not in detail. What happened?"

"You know, if you google Kendall Baylor and Boulder, Colorado, all the news articles will come up. They did another tribute to him a few months ago, on the first anniversary of his death, so there should even be some fairly recent articles. Samantha really doesn't like to talk about things like that, especially at the dinner table."

"Of course, I don't," Samantha interjected. "It's bad enough that I have a brother who's a policeman, who puts his life on the line every day."

"Don't be melodramatic, Samantha. You can't compare what I do to someone who's in the military, on the front lines of defense. Most days I'm trying to find out who stole someone's television. What's that line from *Everybody Loves Raymond*? Robert, my favorite character. 'How's police work? Oh you know, one day you're rescuing a puppy and the next day you're fishing a skull out of a toilet.' Truly, Sami, my life is only on the line every *other* day."

"Anyway, the articles might give you some insight into what Lauren's been through, if you're interested in knowing more about her," Karl said.

"It really isn't my style to cut in on another guy's territory. She's dating someone. I met him."

49

"Samantha mentioned that. I was kind of surprised," Karl said.

Bryan realized that he had already given himself away to his brother-in-law. "And I admit I was kind of disappointed. But the thing is, I got a distinct vibe that she isn't all that committed to him, no matter what your friend may say, Sami."

"Then you've already had a chance to size up the competition," Karl suggested.

"Karl, what are you encouraging?" Samantha protested. "Charlene is a good friend of mine."

He turned to his wife. "I know you like Charlene, but I've never met anyone who exaggerates everything the way she does. You told me yourself it's the reason you invite her to all your Tara Leigh parties, no matter who's hosting them." He did his best imitation of Charlene, affecting a high-pitched female voice. "This cucumber facial changed my life. My skin was like sandpaper. Now people stop me on the street and ask me how I stay so young looking."

Samantha laughed. "What can I say? She's my best customer, especially since her father died and left her with a small fortune."

Karl continued. "In all the years I've known him, I've never seen your brother light up like that at the mention of a woman's name. I say if she isn't married, she's fair game."

"Oh, you're as bad as Bryan! He talks like a policeman. You talk like a hunter."

"You know what I mean." Karl turned to his brother-in-law. "I say 'may the best man win.' See you here Saturday, about 5:30?"

"I'll be there, *without* bells on."

Chapter Nine

Hot Mamma

L auren pulled out her favorite red v-necked sweater, but this time instead of pairing it with jeans, she dressed it up by putting on her nicest pair of black pants. She tried on several pairs of shoes, opting for the new dressy black ankle boots she had recently purchased, knowing that if Lloyd were there, the boots would make her taller than he was. She paused for a moment in front of the mirror, wishing for a brief moment that she could go back in time and tell her self-conscious middle school self to listen to her mother and stop slouching, to be proud of her height. She chose red poinsettia earrings and took a little more time than she usually did with her makeup. She hadn't really made this much of an effort since Kendall had died. Tonight she wanted to look like a woman who was coming back to life.

She surveyed her naturally-curly hair, which had been recently trimmed a couple of inches to shoulder length, glad she had taken the time to get it highlighted again. It was an early Christmas present to herself. She looked in the mirror, wishing Kendall could be there to admire how nice she looked, realizing how long it had been since she'd truly made the effort to look knockout nice. *Who am I supposed to do that for now? So my boys can say "Our mommy is hot!" Right! So who am I doing this for, anyway? Lloyd? I know he'll be there. The only reason I want Lloyd to see me looking this good is so he'll think I'm out of his league.* She smiled at that wicked thought. *Okay, so I'm doing it for me, so I can feel good about me, so that maybe people will stop feeling sorry for me, so Samantha will stop inviting me to TLC make-up parties because I look tired and haggard. Tonight, if anybody brings up my loss, I'm going to change the subject to something happier. If I'm ever going to get past this, I'm going to have to be part of the process.*

Checking to see how her earrings looked with the outfit, she momentarily caught sight of her eyes and realized that no matter how much sparkle and glitz she added to the outside, her sad eyes still told the real story.

In the family room she found her two little boys, where she had left them, sitting stiffly on the sofa, dressed in their church shoes and slacks, white shirts, and one in red and the other in a green sweater vest. She had expected them to be down on the floor playing with any of a number of their toys scattered about or shaking and investigating the presents under the tree. *Maybe I should try this from now on instead of nap time. Get them dressed up and sit them on the sofa like a couple of little miniature mannequins.*

The vests were a gift from Kendall's mother. She loved to dress up her grandchildren. She spoiled her grandsons every bit as much as she spoiled her little granddaughters. "Come on guys. It isn't so bad. I didn't make you wear the bowties. You'll have to wear those to Grammy's house on Christmas, you know."

It had been hard to get used to Kendall's family traditions, especially the ones that were different from her family. She knew that at the family dinner on Christmas day all the little granddaughters would be in red and green velvet dresses, complete with tights, shiny black patent leather shoes and holiday hairbands, all compliments of Grammy. Her first fight with Kendall had been when he had taken her home to meet his extended family during the holidays and hadn't clued her in that they dressed formally for Christmas dinner. She had been woefully underdressed for the occasion and extremely annoyed at her boyfriend for his lack of briefing.

"You guys both look so handsome. It looks like everybody is ready to go to the church. Doesn't Mommy look pretty?" *I need to hear it from someone.* She looked again at her two little boys. Something was off. She was used to Brett's somber face, but why did Dirk look so serious? Suddenly it hit her. The last time someone had dressed them up in new unfamiliar dressy clothes and told them to sit on the sofa until time to go would have been recently when friends and family had planned a memorial tribute on the anniversary of Kendall's death, and of course, there had been that other unhappy day a year before that when lots of sad people had milled around their house, speaking in hushed tones.

Do they remember or understand any of it or are they just normal kids who don't like getting dressed up? Janet had bought new clothes for the boys to wear to Kendall's funeral, so they would look especially nice, outfits Lauren had never been able to put on them again. Personally, she thought putting suit jackets on little boys was overkill. A white shirt and a clip-on tie had been the most she had subjected her sons to up to that point. And where had they gone that sad, confusing day? To the church. Brett had still been tiny, and she didn't know if Dirk remembered much about that day, but somewhere inside it must have registered.

Her heart broke as she realized she might not be the only one who relived things from the past. Tears sprang to her eyes. "We're going to a *party* at the church, a fun party with lots of food, and the Christmas cookies that Mommy made and wouldn't let you eat. And I think Santa is going to be there." Dirk's face changed at that revelation.

"Santa! Then I can ask him if he got my letter." He jumped down off the sofa.

Brett crawled down off the sofa, taking a cue from his brother, walking stiffly in his new Sunday shoes. One day a week hadn't been enough to break them in yet. While she was getting them dressed, she had contemplated letting the boys wear their casual shoes instead, but she had decided that their dressier shoes would keep them from running around as much. Changing her mind now, she grabbed Brett's sneakers. "Come here, Frankenstein. Sit down. Those shoes don't look very comfortable for you." She let Dirk swap his church shoes, too. While she retrieved their winter coats from the closet, Dirk ran to his room and came back with his cardboard daddy.

"Okay, I'm ready."

Lauren sighed. It was one thing for Half-Daddy to come along on quick errands or a trip to the McDonalds drive-up window. She knew Dirk would want to bring him in and prop him up on a seat at the party. She really didn't want the stares and whispers that would result from that, not tonight. "Good idea, honey. Because I've still

53

got some presents in the car from my shopping today and Half-Daddy can guard them while we're at the party."

"Yeah! My Dad's tough, and nobody will steal anything from our car!"

She ruffled his red hair, grateful he had been so easy to manipulate, as she helped him put his coat on. "I'm thinking from now on we should call him 'Car Daddy' because he rides in the car so much." If she could get her son to call him "Car Daddy," she reasoned, she wouldn't have to wince inwardly at the image the words "Half- Daddy" now conjured up for her. And she could use the name as an excuse to leave him inside the car more often.

"Okay. Come on, Car Daddy. Come on, Brett." She watched with amusement as her young son tried to carry his cardboard dad and shepherd his younger brother, both at the same time.

"You hold Brett's hand, and I'll get Car Daddy in his seatbelt." She reached down took the cardboard replica from her son's hand, opening the door to the backseat. "Brett, climb into your car seat." He scrambled across the seat to his car seat. Dirk followed, now tall enough for a booster seat. She strapped the cardboard cutout in the passenger seat up front, which meant she was able to look in the rear view mirror and see the road rather than cardboard Kendall, a good idea on both counts.

As she drove to the church party, gone was the thought that she looked hot. She'd caught another glimpse of her eyes in the rear view mirror. The sadness was even more visible when all she saw was her eyes—and when she had been crying. She bookmarked this episode to discuss with her counselor, about what more she could do to normalize things for the boys. She remembered when she had talked of "getting things back to normal." Her counselor had gently told her that was not possible, that she had to get used to a new normal, but that she got to decide what that new normal looked like. She recalled that she had reacted angrily saying she wanted her normal to include her boys having a father. Again, the counselor had gently suggested that she did have a choice in that regard, that in the future she might choose to try to find a new father for her boys. That suggestion hadn't been terribly welcomed either, even though a small part of her knew it was true. She didn't like her new normal; she wanted her old normal back.

Waiting in the wings, she knew, was a man who hoped it was a very real possibility for them to join their two families. She began to think of Lloyd as she drove the few miles to the church. There were times that she found herself being sympathetic to his situation, and the time he had brought Marie and Katie over to play with the boys had gone well, except for the fact that there was a dearth of girl toys at her house. It had been obvious when she interacted with them how starved they were for a little motherly attention.

Every once in a while, she would begin to entertain the possibility that there was a chance of having a relationship with Lloyd, but then he would do or say something that would annoy her to the core, and she just couldn't get her head around it. And that kiss! She was still angry about the kiss, but beyond her anger, she simply hadn't felt anything she knew she needed to feel. Even if you didn't feel grand passion and have a hormonal rush when someone kissed you, it either felt right or it didn't. Despite what she'd promised her mother about giving Lloyd a chance, she wasn't going to talk herself into a relationship she simply didn't feel right about.

Chapter Ten

Locking Antlers

The walkway to the church was lit by luminaries, paper bags filled with sand with a candle burning inside. When Dirk reached down to touch one and Lauren went in for the save, she discovered they were made of a thin metal crafted to look like paper bags. She made a mental note to keep her eye out for some of those the next time she went to the craft store. She needed something festive. She didn't have any lights on the house, and her tree still stood empty in the middle of the room with the boxes of decorations surrounding it.

It would have been nice to have Kendall around for some of those chores involving ladders and electricity, some of the home repairs that came up, even with a home that was fairly new. It would have been nice to have Kendall around period. She mentally stopped herself. *Yeah, he's not here. He's never going to be here ever again. I can't live the rest of my life as one big pity party. I'm going to go in there and I'm going to have fun.*

Inside, they hung their coats on the racks and headed in the direction of the Christmas music. Dirk made a beeline to a chocolate fountain in the corner of the hall where festive tables were set for dinner. Before Lauren had a chance to greet anyone, she set her container of cookies on the nearest table and was off and running, Brett on her hip, now wishing she'd left Dirk in his uncomfortable church shoes so it would be easier to keep up with him. "Honey, that's for after dinner, for dessert. We have to eat dinner first and . . ." She took him by the hand and turned to find herself staring into the admiring eyes of Lloyd Owens. *He's like a heat-seeking missile.*

"Hi Lloyd." He didn't look pleased to be looking up at her. He was wearing a white shirt, black suit pants and a Christmas tie, a tie that hung to about where his midsection was heaviest. That and a tucked-in shirt emphasized his girth around the middle.

"You look gorgeous tonight, Lauren. I mean, drop-dead gorgeous." He paused, looking up at her. "You didn't seem to me like the kind of vain girl who bought her shoes from the Kardashian Collection, though."

"Um, thanks for the compliment. And the heels on these boots are four inches too short to be from the Kardashians, but I'm impressed, Lloyd, that you're keeping up on your reality television. Hey, I'd love to stop and chat, but I've got to get my cookies to the dessert table." There was something about looking down on Lloyd that made Lauren feel even less inclined to take him seriously.

"Which ones are they? I want to be sure to sample your cooking."

The missing link before you slot me into the vacancy in your family? "They're just chocolate chip cookies made with mint chocolate chips, nothing special." She turned to her oldest son, setting Brett down. "Dirk, hold your brother's hand and come with me and we'll find our cookies and take them to the dessert table and then we'll find a place to sit down."

She felt Lloyd's eyes on her as she retrieved the container of cookies and headed to the church kitchen, knowing somehow that if she turned around she would find Lloyd planted in the middle of the church hall, like Lot's wife who had been turned to a pillar of salt, staring at her backside as she headed to drop off her food assignment. *Maybe I should have worn my baggy sweats. I think I have more than fulfilled my promise to my mother to give him a chance.*

Halfway to the kitchen, she met up with Samantha Bridges. "Lauren, I hope you don't mind, but we saved a place for you and the boys at our table." She pointed in the direction of the table nearest the entrance, where Lauren could see Samantha's husband Karl and a tall man with his back to her whose hair was a shade or two darker than hers. "That's my brother, Bryan. And he wants to meet you, when he's *not* wearing a Santa suit."

"What?" Suddenly the light went on and her face turned an appropriate shade of red. "Ohhh. I'm sorry. I didn't know who . . ."

"It's okay. I told him I might have done the same thing under the circumstances. He was actually impressed that you were so vigilant," Samantha said.

"Okay, let me drop off these cookies, and we'll be right over."

Lauren glanced in Lloyd's direction as she headed toward Samantha's table and saw that from his seat, he was following her every move. She was sure he expected her to come over and sit by him and the girls, but she reasoned it would also have been rude if she were to brush off Samantha's invitation. She gave a little wave to Charlene, seated with her husband and children at the next table over from Lloyd, hoping Charlene would not be hurt if she didn't come sit near them. She was glad Kendall's parents were off visiting his sister that weekend, so she didn't have the further awkwardness of choosing to meet a new man rather than sit with her in-laws.

Bryan stood and turned around as Samantha introduced him to Lauren. She let go of Brett's hand for a moment and extended her hand, remembering self-consciously that she was wearing the same red sweater as she had worn the day he'd attempted to play Santa. Before he could grasp her hand in greeting, two little girls each grabbed one of her arms. "Lauren, come sit with us. Pleeeease! We want you and Dirk and Brett to sit with us. We saved you some seats. Pleeease!"

"Nice to meet you, Bryan." It was nice to look up at a man again, for a change. She remembered his eyes. She'd looked into those eyes before, even if they had been surrounded by a beard and white hair. Tonight they were set off by a navy-blue pullover sweater with a layer of tan in the ribbing around the neck. The sweater made his eyes look blue. She remembered them as gray. The tan ribbing perfectly set off his thick light-brown hair. It was definitely an improvement over the Santa wig and beard. But it seemed eye contact was going to be all they got this time around, too. Feeling like a turkey wishbone about to be split in half, she shot him an apologetic look as the two little girls dragged her across the room to a table where a triumphant Lloyd sat, a self-satisfied smile on his face.

Lauren situated the boys on either side of her, across from Lloyd, who had a daughter on either side of him, leaving one vacant seat next to Marie. He looked a little too pleased with himself and it annoyed Lauren immensely. She suspected he had engineered the girls pulling her away from her introduction to Bryan, but she could hardly disappoint his two little girls. She looked across the table at the three of them, all with the same dark hair and brown eyes. *Their mother must have dark hair, too. I wonder if she has regrets, not spending the holidays with her little girls. Surely they must have some sort of arrangement for her to see them occasionally, even if he has full custody. I'll have to ask him about that sometime.*

Bryan looked over his shoulder as Lauren seated herself at Lloyd's table. "Someone made short work of that introduction."

"I'm sorry about that, Bry," Samantha said. "And after I was willing to let the cat out of the bag about the service project for your sake."

"And I appreciate that, Sami. I do." He smiled. "And don't say that in front of the little redheaded guy, about the cat in the bag, because if he hears that a second time, I'll probably have to scare up a Christmas kitten."

"We can find a stuffed one," she offered. "Anyway, at least now maybe you can make another Santa run."

"I intend to." He stood up. "Right now."

After a blessing on the food, it was announced that they would be accessing the Christmas buffet one table at a time to avoid a stampede. The table nearest the entrance was invited up.

"Which table are we, Mom?" Dirk asked, looking enviously at all the people from the first table filling their plates. "What if all that dripping chocolate is gone?"

"We're table number four, the same number as how old you are. And see that lady over there by the chocolate fountain? Her job is to make sure they don't run out of chocolate. But I'll have to help you, because that can be really messy. We have to keep your Christmas vests nice so we can wear them to Grammy's house."

60

He sighed. "Christmas has too much waiting."

"I hear you, buddy." Bryan Everett set his green plastic plate down next to Marie and across from Dirk. It contained only a green salad and a couple of side dishes, because he hadn't wanted to take the chance that someone else might take the one vacant seat left at Lauren's table.

He caught her eye. "Our introduction was interrupted, so I thought I would come join you at your table. It appears this seat is vacant. You don't mind, do you?"

Before she could answer, Lloyd piped up. "Isn't that cheating? If you get served first for sitting at table one, I think you're *supposed to sit* at table one."

"You're so right. And I'm nothing if not a law-abiding citizen. If security comes around for the check, I'll go back." He repeated his question, this time looking straight at Lauren. "*You* don't mind, do you?" Her mind raced. *Okay, I told him Lloyd was my boyfriend, so now if I flirt with him, I look like a two-timer. Worse, because I would be flirting with him in front of my boyfriend. But Lloyd doesn't know this is the guy in the Santa suit, so he doesn't know that Bryan thinks he is supposedly my boyfriend, so Bryan can flirt with me. And Bryan is obviously making a point of sitting here and wants to get better acquainted, so if I'm polite but not flirtatious, neither of them should have a problem with it.*

"No, I don't mind," she said. "No one was sitting there, right Lloyd?"

Bryan looked at Lloyd and smiled. "I know *you* mind." He turned his attention back to Lauren. "I thought you might need some help with the little guys. Juggling three plates can't be easy."

"And *I'm* here to help her," Lloyd said.

"I'm sure you are, but you've got your two little girls here to look out for, haven't you?"

"They're old enough to handle their own plates."

Bryan smiled. "But that chocolate fountain could be tricky." He turned his attention back to Lauren. "So where were we? You're Lauren, of course, but I already knew that. And I'm Bryan." He extended his hand again, this time finding hers free.

61

"And these are your little boys. Samantha told me their names, but I want to make sure I get it right this time."

"This is Dirk and the little guy is Brett."

He turned to the little girl next to him. "And what's your name?"

She turned to her father as though for approval to talk to a stranger and then turned back to him. "I'm Marie."

"And your sister?"

"Her name is Kathleen, but we call her Katie."

"And this must be dear old dad." He extended his hand. "Bryan Everett. You may or may not know my sister, Samantha."

"I'm Lloyd Owens." He took the extended hand with a scowl. "No, I don't really know your sister. We're new here."

"Oh, and where are you from?"

"Boca Raton, Florida." From the tone Lloyd used declaring the upscale city that had been his former residence, Lauren knew no sob stories about a lost job and the near-foreclosure on a home would be forthcoming. "I was in research and development at Motorola."

In exchange, Bryan pulled out something he had hoped to bring up in a more subtle way to Lauren, knowing that his profession had gotten in the way of more than one romance along the way and could be especially troubling to a woman who had suffered a recent loss and might not be interested in a man with a dangerous profession. "I'm with the Boulder Police Department. You can call me *Sergeant* Everett."

"I feel safer already," Lloyd said dryly.

Dirk was fascinated. "You're a policeman?"

Seated within earshot on the other side of Katie, Charlene joined the conversation. "Lloyd is now working with my husband, the owner of Colorado Heights Construction. He's heading up the remodel on the McAllister Mansion, the old bed and breakfast in El Dorado Springs. It's going to be simply breathtaking when it's finished."

"That's a bit of a switch, from research and development to construction," Bryan observed.

"It was time for a change. I've always been good at building things."

"Was your father a builder?" Lauren asked.

"One of them. My parents divorced when I was a baby. My mother married Charlene's dad when I was two, but they divorced when I was ten. My mother remarried again when I was thirteen, so yeah, my second step-father taught me how to build. He was a contractor."

Listening to Lloyd's "Tale of Three Fathers" made Lauren even more determined not to make any mistakes regarding the next man she brought into her life and into the life of her little boys. She had not missed a look that had been exchanged between Charlene and Ryan when Charlene said Lloyd was managing the B & B restoration. In the brief time she'd known Charlene, she had noticed that she tended to embellish things when it suited her purposes. From the look on Ryan's face, she judged that Lloyd had been given an unauthorized promotion by his sister.

Lloyd wasn't done. "And now I'm honored to share the humble profession of carpenter with my Lord and Saviour, whose birth we celebrate this holy time of year."

Lauren looked at Sergeant Everett to see his reaction to Lloyd's pious declaration. He raised a forkful of chestnut dressing in the air. "And I am likewise honored to have the job of separating the wheat from the tares."

Charlene jumped into the conversation again. "We're just so grateful after all Phil—Lloyd . . ." She made a quick recovery, turning to Lloyd. "There I go again, confusing you with Uncle Floyd."

Bryan couldn't resist. "Must be the protruding nose hairs."

Lauren was usually looking across at Lloyd, or down at him if she was in heels, not up at him, but upon investigation Bryan was right. Lloyd's nose hairs *were* in serious need of trimming. Charlene shot Bryan a dirty look. "Like I was saying, after *all* Lloyd's been through, we are *so* grateful that he has found a woman like Lauren to date who is *such* a good mother." She turned to Lauren. "Your boys are *so* well behaved. Why Brett hasn't made a peep!"

Bryan didn't take the bait. He looked at Lauren's frozen smile and sensed the balance of power had somehow just tipped in his direction. "I can see that already, and I've only known her for such a short time."

A quick announcement came over the mike. "Table four." Lauren was grateful for the reprieve, hoping Lloyd and Bryan could get their antlers untangled long enough for everyone to get some food.

The rest of the evening continued in much the same vein. When Samantha saw Lauren head to the ladies' room, with a dancing Brett in tow, she was right behind. Lauren was not surprised to see Bryan's sister washing her hands at the sink next to her. She knew how women worked, that Sami was there for the update. Lauren also knew that anything she said could and would be repeated back to Sergeant Everett. She was just grateful that her mother was in Italy and not calling for daily reports, or worse, showing up in person to meddle.

"So, are you getting to know Bryan? I apologize again for sending him over in the Santa suit without letting you know he was coming. I—we—just wanted to do something special for you on the sly. By the way, your hair looks great. Did you do something different? I think you blew my brother out of the water tonight."

She squirted soap onto her little boy's hands and lifted him up to the faucet to rinse his hands. "Oh, he must think this is the only sweater I own. I think this is what I was wearing when he came by playing Santa, only I was wearing it with jeans."

"You're rockin' it tonight." Sami dangled yet another fishing line. "If you ask me, it looks like you've got the attention of more than just Bryan . . ."

"Tell me about it." Lauren paused. "Two guys competing for me over dinner. What more could a girl want for Christmas?" She grabbed a couple of paper towels and handed them to Brett to dry his hands. "Have you ever thought that hell could be like being eternally in high school? I waited forever for the guys to be taller than I am, which finally happened. But waiting for them to be more mature . . ."

Samantha laughed. "Testosterone poisoning."

"Big time at table four tonight. I'm just cutting up meat for my boys while Lloyd and Bryan cut each other down to size. I know there's probably entertainment planned for tonight, but honestly, they're providing all I need. Do you really think they imagine that whoever has the most points at the end of the night gets me, like I don't have any choice in the matter?"

Samantha laughed again. "I'm having a flashback to Karl talking to my old boyfriend at my 20th class reunion."

"So you know what I'm talking about?"

"Oh, totally! So would you mind if I sent Bryan back over with the toys, say early next Saturday evening, around five or six?"

"Sure, now that I know who he is. My boys are going to have Santa overkill this season. Isn't there a Santa coming at the end of the evening?" Lauren asked.

"Actually, I heard that they're having the three wise men visit, giving each family a new star for the top of their tree."

"Oh, that's a good idea. The kids need a reminder of what it's all about. For that matter, the grown-ups need a reminder, too. I told Dirk Santa was coming, but now I know so I can prepare him ahead of time for a change in plans to the wise men. It will be great if I can tell him that Santa is making an early visit on Saturday. We, um I, got a plastic nativity for the little boys last year, so they know the wise men. Knowing Dirk he'll want to know where their camels are."

"Outside eating carrots with the reindeer, right?"

"Good one! I'll have to remember that."

"I'm glad you got a chance to meet Bryan outside of the Santa suit. Outside of his police uniform, too, for that matter. Sometimes I tease him for talking like a cop. One time I was disciplining one of my kids for something and he called him 'the perp.'"

Lauren laughed as she pulled a couple more paper towels out of the dispenser for her own hands. "Well, back to see if Comet and Cupid are still locking antlers."

While Lloyd waited outside the ladies' room for his little girls, Bryan saw that Lauren was getting ready to head out, and he made his move, offering to walk her to the car. "Do you think he would mind if I carried him?" he asked, referring to little Brett, whose energy was long since spent.

"I know *I* wouldn't mind if you carried him. I was going to wait until we got outside before I picked him up. He's practically asleep, so I'm sure he probably won't even know who's carrying him. Thanks! I think I got all the chocolate off his face, but watch your sweater, just in case."

Bryan lifted the little boy up, and Brett immediately laid his head on his shoulder and fell the rest of the way asleep. "Wow! That was fast."

"When he decides to fall asleep, he just does it. As a baby, he used to fall asleep in the middle of a feeding. And more than once as a toddler, he's face-planted in his dinner."

"Time to try some new recipes?"

She laughed. "That's got to be what it is. My cooking just isn't exciting enough."

Bryan opened the door with his free hand, letting Lauren and Dirk through first. Lauren bent down and examined one of the luminaries. "I wonder where they got these. They're cool."

"Aren't they just paper bags with sand and candles?" Bryan asked

"No, these ones are metal but made to look like paper bags. And they have built-in candle holders, so you just put a little tea light in."

"Oh, so you don't need as much sand to stabilize the bag. Good idea." He shifted the little boy to the other shoulder. "So Dirk, show me the ornament you got."

Dirk held up the golden star. "That's going to look great on your Christmas tree."

"Maybe it will motivate me to put up the rest of the ornaments," Lauren said.

They reached her car and Bryan placed Brett in his car seat, letting Lauren take it from there.

"I'd give it a try, but car seats are all so different . . ."

"Carrying him was help enough, trust me. Thank you."

"I never trust anyone who says 'trust me.'" He hesitated a moment, enjoying the smile she graced him with at that remark. "I'm kind of embarrassed at how I acted in there. I didn't mean to let my ego take over. I was actually hoping to bring up my profession in a more tactful way."

This time Lauren laughed out loud, wondering how long it had been since she'd heard the sound of her own spontaneous laughter. "Instead of the next round of 'can you top this?' with Lloyd."

"What could I pull out after his *humble carpenter* shtick?"

She laughed again. "I don't mean to bring up minor details, but you pulled out the 'Sergeant Everett' *before* Lloyd's declaration about being a humble carpenter."

"Guilty as charged," Bryan admitted. "I guess that changes everything."

As she bent over to begin buckling Brett into his car seat, Bryan posed a question.

"So Lauren, could I give you a call sometime?"

She fumbled with the buckles on the car seat as she answered his question, not sure what her answer would be if she risked more eye contact with the handsome police sergeant. "You know, I'm really not dating yet. It isn't that I wouldn't like to hear from you, Bryan. You seem like someone I'd like to know better." She smiled, finished with her task, and turned to face him. "I'm sorry. You wanted a phone number, not commentary."

"I'm pretty sure I didn't want a 'you're a nice guy but' speech. Forgive me for asking, but I do need to clarify something. This Lloyd guy, when I stopped by in the Santa suit and he showed up. I can tell he's interested in you, and you said he was . . ."

"I said he was my boyfriend. And just now I said I'm not dating. And who knows what anyone thought at dinner tonight, especially the kids. Confusing, right? And the pathetic part is that I'm the most confused of everybody. We'd been on one date, a set-up. He just showed up that night, as he often does now that he's staying at his sister's house nearby. I didn't know who you were, so I made up a little white lie to get rid of you, or to make it seem like there was a man in my life. It was out of self-protection. I'm sorry. I'm really not one of those game players, although that is what it certainly must seem like."

"I get that. Apology accepted." He paused. "Okay, so you *are* available then? And by that I mean, not dating but not in a relationship either."

She closed the door on her car, mostly to keep the boys warm, but also so that the rest of her conversation with Bryan could be private. "I'm definitely *not* dating Lloyd. Sometimes I'm not sure yet that *he* knows we're not dating, but we're not. It's the timing, really. I'm still picking up the pieces . . ." He saw the sadness return to her eyes. "You know, until you lose someone, you don't realize how many figures of speech are going to haunt you. I never thought twice about saying 'I could die' over something like a bad hair day or saying 'I'm going to kill him when he gets home.'" She lowered her head. "I'm still very much trying to come back to life after losing my husband. Anyone who wants to have a relationship with me is going to need the patience of Job. I've been getting these weird phone calls, so I'm probably a little more paranoid than I normally would be, so I've been kind of wary about sharing my . . ."

He fished a card from his wallet and scribbled another number on the bottom. "How's this? No pressure. Here's my card. I put my cell phone number on there. Easy to remember 246-8007. Two Four Six Eight. Who do we appreciate? And Double O Seven, like James Bond. Don't call the other number unless you have a crime to report. I don't give this number out too often, either, but for different reasons than you, I suppose. I'm just sort of anti-social."

"What? No tweets every fifteen seconds?" Lauren asked.

"Not likely." Bryan looked into her eyes. He could not help drinking in the depths of the sad, guarded eyes of this intriguing woman. "Red and green. Very Christmassy."

"What?"

"Your eyes and your sweater. Sorry, I couldn't help noticing." He paused. "Why do I suddenly feel like I'm fifteen?"

She laughed. "Except for the two kids, I'm right there with you. Maybe it's awkward getting acquainted at any age."

"Could be. I hope I don't remain single long enough to discover that the hard way, unsuccessfully hitting on the woman in the next room over at the nursing home." He smiled. "So if you'd ever like to get together, or if you just need someone to talk to, you can give me a call, on your schedule and on your timetable." He paused. "I might be able to help you figure out who's making the phone calls. Feel free to call me about that and I'll see what I can do."

"Oh, thank you. And thanks for understanding," Lauren said.

He noticed the cardboard cutout sitting in her front seat. "This must be your husband, still watching over his family. Either that, or you're using him as an excuse to illegally drive in the carpool lane."

"I guess you always have to be thinking like a police officer." She smiled. "Dirk is very attached to this one. It goes pretty much everywhere with him. I'm starting to get some flack about it now and then, from a few people. It's progress that he lets it stay in the car."

"If it makes him feel better, I wouldn't worry about what anyone else thinks."

She smiled again, and this one went all the way to her eyes. "Thank you, Bryan. Thank you for saying that. You know, when my boys fall down and scrape their knee or something, I used to try to get them to stop crying."

"I know the drill. 'Big boys don't cry,'" he said.

"Exactly! Now I tell them to cry until it feels better," she said.

"I can tell that you're a mother who puts the needs of her kids ahead of her own. There are a lot of selfish women out there. The last woman I dated was two of them." He grinned, and Lauren noticed that his eyes crinkled when he smiled. "I just want to tell you I think you're doing a great job and you don't have to listen to anybody else's drive-by opinion. You're the one who knows your boys best."

"Thank you! And thank you for an enjoyable and entertaining evening. After sitting with you and Lloyd, the real entertainment was kind of secondary. I'm glad you came and sat at our table, even if it did make things a little awkward. I'm glad to have met the man inside the suit."

"So my sister tells me I'll be stopping by next Saturday evening, about dusk, with the bag of toys. Is that still, okay?"

"We're planning on it. See you Saturday, Santa."

"I've been told women can't resist a man in uniform."

She smiled. "Then it looks like you've got it covered either way."

Chapter Eleven

Scavenging a Suit

From the side door into the church, Lloyd watched angrily as Bryan walked Lauren to her car, carrying Brett. His sister was soon beside him. "Did you have a good time?"

"I did until *that* guy showed up. I don't know who he is. He talked like he had met Lauren before and yet she acted like it was the first time she'd met him. I don't get it." He turned angrily to his youngest daughter. "Couldn't you have just held it until we got home?"

Katie looked like she was about to cry. Charlene jumped in. "Don't take it out on her, Lloyd."

He was still staring at Lauren and Bryan. "Oh, great! He's giving her his card. 'Call me if you need anything. I'm a big strong police sergeant and I'll be there within thirty seconds with my lights flashing and my siren blaring.' Things were going so well. I really didn't need this complication. If Amber should ever make another bid for custody sometime down the line for whatever reason, my chances of keeping the girls for good would be so much better if I could show that they have a wonderful new caring mother and a stable home life."

Charlene smiled. "You can't force it, Lloyd, but I do have a little information that might be helpful."

"Oh yeah? What's that?"

"My friend Diane was in the restroom and overheard Samantha, Bryan's sister, talking to Lauren. She knows I introduced you to Lauren. I told her about your dinner out. She said something about him playing Santa and coming over to her house, again."

"Again? Wait! *He's* the Santa she wouldn't let in!" He paused. "It all makes sense now. *He* knew who *she* was but *she* didn't recognize *him*."

"Early next Saturday evening, that's when he's going over, around five."

"Then I'll just have to get there first. And that means I've got a week to score a Santa suit. I'll be home soon. I told this guy I met, an old friend of Lauren's husband, that I'd help with the cleanup. Do you mind taking the girls back home with you?"

Back at the house, Lloyd began his online search for a Santa suit. After a few minutes, he slammed shut the lid of his laptop computer, discouraged. "You'd think that somewhere in the greater Denver area there would be at least *one* Santa suit for sale!"

Charlene looked up from the nearby sofa. "It *is* that time of year. It isn't something stores want to overstock. You wouldn't be caught dead in a Santa suit in February."

"Thanks for the fashion tip, Char," he said sarcastically. "There are places where I could mail-order one, but the nice ones are way more expensive than I'd expected. Amber didn't spend that much on her wedding gown. And to get it here by Saturday, I'd have to pay for expedited shipping, too."

"I suppose I *could help* you out with some money if . . ."

"That's very generous of you. I'd accept your offer, but I don't want Ryan to blow his stack. He's already not very happy about our little pay arrangement. He told me yesterday that he agreed to do it because he thought it would only be for a few weeks, until I found something else, that he didn't know this was going to turn into a long-term arrangement."

"Don't worry about Ryan. I can handle him."

"I can only imagine how happy he'd be if he knew you tapped out your entire Christmas shopping budget subsidizing a Santa suit."

"You're probably right," Charlene said. "He doesn't deal well with what he considers unnecessary expenditures. And I never talk with him about things like this in the evening. He's always in a better mood after he's had a good night's sleep."

"I'll keep looking. I haven't tried e-bay yet. Maybe someone local has a suit I could buy and pick up in person." A few minutes later he closed the computer again with a sigh. "There are a couple of suits available in the area, but they're on auctions that don't end before Saturday, so that you'll pay the higher 'Buy-it Now' prices that reflect the seller's willingness to take advantage of someone else's desperation, in this case, mine."

Charlene put down her book as an idea came to her. "Freecycle! Have you ever heard of that? Sometimes when we have leftover materials from a remodel, Ryan will put things like an old sink or tub on Freecycle and somebody comes and takes it off our hands. We have an account. I'll pull that up for you and you can see if by chance there is someone out there tired of playing Santa. It's worth a try, huh?"

A few minutes later Lloyd hit pay dirt. He hurriedly scribbled down the phone number, not wanting to wait for the exchange of an email. "If I hurry, it's not too late to call and maybe I can pick it up tomorrow."

* * *

Lloyd drove slowly through the mobile home park, looking for number 1382. He drove past 1380 and the next house number was 138. On closer examination, he saw the 2, dangling from just one nail, partially obscured by the bare branch of a tree. He stopped the car and made his way up the walk, past a collection of random junk piled haphazardly on the small porch. He knocked on the door with barely room to stand between the piles. *These must be the people who have been taking all the old sinks and tubs and used doorknobs that Ryan gives away.*

An overweight lady in grey sweatpants and a stretched-out oversized yellow sweater answered the door. She had a large plastic poinsettia flower bobby-pinned in her reddish-brown hair. "Ya here for the Santa suit?"

Lloyd nodded. "Yes, I am." From what he could see, the inside of the house was as full of clutter as the porch, perhaps even more so.

She grabbed a heavy-duty black garbage bag. "My ex was a smoker, so ya might wanna Febreze this before ya wear it. I checked and it's all there—suit, belt, beard, hat, boots." She smiled a gap-toothed smile. "Cleanin' house. He was the first piece of junk I offloaded. Now I'm gettin' rid of all his crap."

Lloyd wordlessly took the black bag from her and then remembered his manners. "Thank you and, um, Merry Christmas."

"Yeah. Sure. Whatever."

He wasn't sure he dared look inside the bag, but the price was right. He stuffed it into the backseat of the car Charlene had so graciously offered to let him drive while he was in town. He had a few days to air the suit out. A Santa suit was a Santa suit. The important thing was that he arrive at Lauren's house the following Saturday before Sergeant Bryan Everett, aka Santa.

Chapter Twelve

Back Off

As unnerving as it could be, Lauren was getting used to Lloyd's pop-in visits. She found it hard to scold him in front of his children, and in the evenings, he often brought them along to play with the boys when he stopped by. She wasn't surprised when he showed up on Sunday, the morning after the Christmas party.

At the knock on her front door, she invited the three of them in. The girls hurried into the family room off the kitchen and joined Dirk and Brett who were watching cartoons in their pajamas. "What's up?"

"Sorry to come by without calling, like you asked me to do. I tried your cell phone, but it must not be charged up."

"No, I think it's charged. And I think I left it in the car," Lauren said. "Lloyd, it's Sunday morning. It's a little early to . . ."

"I have a favor to ask of you."

"A favor?"

He followed her into the family room and sat down on the sofa. Lauren, as usual, sat as far away from him as she could. "The girls are out of school for the holidays starting Monday, and my sister has been so good to us that I really didn't want to ask another thing of her," Lloyd said. "This time of year she's on the run a lot, shopping, overseeing one of the businesses her father left her, and her teen-agers don't want to be stuck babysitting my girls. I was hoping this could be a win-win situation." Lloyd looked around the room. "I figure you probably have a few handyman things that need to be done since you're without a man around the house, and I need someone to babysit my girls during the day while I work. Of course, I won't need you on the weekends."

"This is really kind of last minute, Lloyd. You're really putting me on the spot here."

"I know. I know. I should have thought of it before. It just didn't occur to me what an imposition it would be on my sister after she's already done so much for me."

Immediately the two little girls were by her side, in a repeat performance of the Christmas party. "Pleeease, Lauren! Your house is lots funner than Aunt Charlene's. Our cousins don't like it when we go in their rooms. And they're too old for The Disney Channel." Little Katie looked up at her and Lauren found it hard to resist the pleading big brown eyes. "Will you teach me how to make cookies?"

Lauren sighed. "I got the leak on my kitchen faucet spray nozzle fixed, but the wood under the sink is warped now. I could use some help replacing that and now that you mention it, I guess there are a few other . . ."

"Why don't you make a list of all the things you need me to do. I'll get the supplies and we'll hook you up," Lloyd said.

"The kids do play well together. Do they have some of their toys they can bring over so they won't be bored with all the boy toys?"

"A lot of our stuff is in storage right now, since we're in such a small place, but we can bring a few things over."

"I'm *not* playing Barbies," Dirk said.

"My mom never let us have Barbies. She said . . ."

Lloyd quickly cut Katie off. "They've got a couple of baby dolls. But honestly, they told me how much fun they had with the blocks and puzzles over here, and as Marie said, there's always The Disney Channel."

"Dirk and Brett's other parent."

"I hear you there," he said. He turned to his girls. "Speaking of The Disney Channel, it looks like Dirk has it on right now. Maybe you can watch it for a few minutes while I talk to Dirk and Brett's mommy." The girls plopped down on the rug next to Dirk, who had half a cardboard daddy propped up next to him, with a tie loosely draped around his neck.

"So your cardboard dad watches television with you, too, Dirk?" Lloyd asked.

"He does everything with me. He's already ready for church. See, he's got his tie on."

Lloyd turned to Lauren taking her by the arm and leading her into the kitchen. "You're not going to let him take that thing to church, are you?" he whispered.

"Sometimes I do. Sometimes I don't. And none of us are going to church if you don't get out of here and let us get ready. That *thing* happens to be all he has left of his father. Cardboard Kendall attended his own funeral, so everybody at church is used to seeing him now and then. Sure, we're hoping to get him down to being one of those infrequent churchgoers, but for now . . ."

Lloyd shook his head. "If you want my opinion . . ."

She cut him off at the knees. "I don't. I pay a counselor big bucks to discuss things like this, one I trust and whose advice I follow." *Someone who doesn't have his own agenda.* "I'm not going to discuss it with you or anyone else for that matter. Believe me, you're not the only one with an opinion about it."

"I just thought you might want a man's viewpoint."

"My counselor is a man."

"Oh." He stopped short. "For some reason I thought you were seeing a female counselor."

"What difference does that make? A skilled counselor is a skilled counselor."

"It just seems like when you talk about the counsel you get that . . ."

"That it seems like counsel I would get from a *woman*? Newsflash! There *are* men out there who are sensitive and understanding. The female gender doesn't have a corner on those traits."

"Is this guy single?"

She began to unload the dishwasher while they talked, angrily putting plates and glasses back into the cupboard. "What difference could that possibly make? And what business would it be of yours? Are you implying that I have something going with my counselor?"

"A lot of women develop crushes on their shrinks."

"That may be, but if the guy has any professional ethics, he doesn't respond. I have no idea, for the record. We don't talk about *his* life. We talk about *mine*."

"Women tend to become dependent on men they lean on and sometimes it turns romantic. You're more vulnerable right now than you realize, Lauren. For example, that police sergeant the other night. That's the kind of man a vulnerable woman might find herself drawn toward for all the wrong reasons. I couldn't help but notice you have his card on your bulletin board."

"He said he might be able to help me track down who's been making those phone calls, not that it's any of *your* business." She waved a handful of silverware in his face. "Now that you've warned me about being vulnerable, I'll be more careful. I guess we ought to rethink this whole thing about you doing repairs for me then, in case I start to depend on you. Maybe I should just have you pay me for the babysitting."

"But you need . . . Don't you want . . .?"

"That's right. I could use some things done. And you think you're just going to come over here with your box of tools and fix a couple of things and I'll fall right into your arms. You're warning me about being vulnerable and at the same time you're counting on it." She held up her left hand. "See this. It's my wedding ring. I took it off for that date with you, one of the hardest things I've ever had to do, and I'm not talking about having to grease it up with butter to get it off. It is *back on*. And what that means to you, or any other guy right now, including Sergeant Everett, is *back off!* When you see that this ring is no longer on my finger, it means I've decided to start dating. Now if you meant what you said about us being mutually supportive of each other, then stop acting like the understudy waiting in the wings for the leading man to get the bubonic plague."

"I'm sorry. I can't help but think you're all avoiding reality. You're still wearing your wedding rings. You have cardboard cutouts of your dead husband all over the house. The one in your bedroom window is especially intimidating."

"*What?* When have you been in my backyard? I keep that big wooden gate latched and closed. You can only see that one from the backyard." He'd either been in her backyard or her bedroom, and she wasn't happy about either of those possibilities.

"Calm down. You know that wild cat and her kittens you've been feeding. I came over one afternoon and you weren't here. I saw her around by the back of your garage. I remembered that I had some beef jerky in my pocket, so I followed her around and let myself through the gate and tried to lure her into your garage with the beef jerky, because I know you keep food there for her. Isn't that why you leave the garage door open a little bit? The gate wasn't latched, by the way, but I could help you get a more secure lock on it if you seriously want to keep people out of your backyard. Anyway, I looked up and there he was in the window, staring me down." He hesitated and changed the subject. "Hey, how about if I hook you up with a pet door in the side door to your garage?"

Lauren felt herself start to calm down. She stopped unloading the dishwasher and rattling the dishes. "Okay, I'm sorry I got so worked up just now. Anything having to do with my privacy is kind of a hot button."

"I get that. I'm just glad you calmed down before you got to the sharp knives."

"Very funny!" She smiled weakly. "That's actually a good idea. I could leave the bed and the food inside the side door and leave a trail of food leading up to the pet door and she'd probably figure it out."

"Then you wouldn't have to leave your garage door partially open like you've been doing. It would be safer. You know, anyone could come along and open your garage the way you're doing it now."

"The door is so noisy going up, I haven't really worried about anyone opening it without me knowing about it. I only leave it open during the day. I haven't really got much in there worth stealing. We go in and out through the garage and then we don't make a mess coming in through the front door. The boys can leave their boots in the garage by the door into the house. But speaking of being safer, I have been meaning to get a deadbolt installed on the door from the garage into the house. Is that something you could help me with?"

"Sure. I know the best brand. I'll pick one up when I pick up the wood for under your sink."

"Okay." She hesitated and took a deep breath. "I think this can work." Lloyd was becoming more likable again, but she wondered how long it would be before he would annoy her again. If he did repairs for her, he couldn't make her feel obligated to date him, because he was getting something of value in return. It was a business arrangement. On the one hand, she knew she was being played. When Katie had looked up at her and asked if they could make cookies, Lauren had been reasonably sure that line had been fed to her in advance.

She didn't doubt that Lloyd would use Marie and Katie to good advantage, to play on her desire to mother daughters as well as sons. The two little girls were well behaved, sometimes too well behaved. Lauren had noticed that they often looked to their father before or after they spoke, seemingly for permission or confirmation. On the other hand, she wasn't sure if Lloyd had thought about this, but he would be leaving his little girls unscripted in her company for the better part of the day every weekday for a couple of weeks, something that was sure to be illuminating.

Chapter Thirteen

Phoney Baloney

After church Lloyd dropped the girls at his sister's house. "Do you mind if I leave the girls here for a while? I've got a friend I need to visit. He's going through a bad breakup, like I did, and I really want to be there for him."

Charlene touched his arm. "Oh, that's good of you. Sure. Go ahead. We were going to watch *Miracle on 34th Street* this afternoon, so that ought to entertain them."

"Great! They'll love that. Thanks, Char."

* * *

Lloyd pulled up at the El Dorado Bed and Breakfast Bed and Breakfast, rubbing his hands together to stay warm. A few minutes later a beat-up tan Chevy pick-up pulled up and Jason Bremmer got out.

"What's up? Why'd you drag me all the way down here?"

"Because I don't want to be seen with you anywhere but our workplace," Lloyd said.

"Let's at least go inside and stay warm."

Lloyd opened the door and they went inside the spacious foyer. Jason sat down in an ornate chair which was covered by a drop cloth.

"No need to make yourself at home. This won't take long."

"Good, because there's a game on I wanna see. So wassup?" Jason asked.

"We've got to be more careful. There's someone starting to snoop around, a cop. There are ways to trace what cell phone tower calls come from. Have you made all the calls from around here? He knows I'm working on this El Dorado renovation."

Jason looked confused. "I thought you said the phone was untraceable."

"The *ownership* can't be tracked, but the location of the calls can. The longer you talk, the better chance of triangulating the call. The guy's a police officer. He could pinpoint a location and radio in and have the nearest cop be on the lookout for somebody suspicious talking on a cell phone. We've got to be more careful, that's all. Look Jason, I've kept you in drug money while you helped me out with this, but I can't take a chance on being found out. I've got too much at stake. Maybe we should just stop with the calls."

"Come on, I'm just getting good at this. Lauren and me, we got a thing going."

"No you *don't,* you moron! At first she turned to me for comfort, like I'd planned, but she might also turn to that police sergeant, which just could be my undoing."

"Yeah, one of these days she might put it together that you always showed up right after I called so you could comfort her. So have you got any hot pictures of this babe, because I'd really like to see what she looks like, if she's worth all the . . ."

"No, I haven't got any hot pictures of her. She's not like that. And if I did, I wouldn't show them to a lowlife like you," Lloyd said.

"Hey, I've got an idea!" Jason said. "You could plant the phone, you know, in his car or somewhere that she would find it, make it look like *he's* the one with a friend making the calls to make her feel scared and stuff."

"Let me see that phone." Lloyd flipped it open and pulled up the log of calls placed. Lauren's number came up several times and then his number showed up. "Okay, Einstein. That's like the guy who was his own defense lawyer and asked the victim, 'Did you get a good look at my face when I took your purse?' You've called *me* a bunch of times from this phone, to report in that you had called her so I'd know when to go over and comfort her. Planting it in his truck would be giving him the missing piece of evidence he needs to tie me to the phantom caller."

"Sorry, man. I wasn't thinking."

"You're a lot smarter when you're high." Suddenly the light went on. "Wait! What if there was another phone that incriminated *him* the same way this one incriminates me? She has a business card with his cell phone number on her bulletin board at her house, so getting that is no problem. I'll buy another phone, you can call her from that one, only this time make the calls close to the precinct where he works. Then every once in a while make a call to *his* cell number. Then I can be the hero who helps trace the calls and helps her see that the clues all point to him."

"What'll I say when I call him?"

"Try to sell him something. Pretend it's a wrong number and apologize. Just keep him on the line long enough so that it registers as a call that was made. After we've got enough calls on the phone in the recent memory, I'll plant that one. It won't take that many calls. Then *he'll* look like he orchestrated it all to get close to her, all the while comforting her and pretending to help her to throw her off the track." Lloyd continued. "Reverse reverse psychology. And I'll be there, helping her connect the dots."

"You scare me, dude."

"I'm so brilliant I sometimes scare myself. Give me that phone, and I'll have a replacement one to you by tomorrow. I'll make sure it's got a few pictures of her home and kids on it, too."

Jason had another question. "But what about the fact that I've been calling her before she ever met him? How are you going to make that fit?"

"I don't know, but I'll think of something. He knew who she was, used his sister to get an introduction. Who would know better how to be an undercover stalker than a police officer?"

Chapter Fourteen

Sleep Tight

Lauren was propped up in bed, her reading lamp softly illuminating the pages of *Speedbumps,* the book by Teri Garr that she was still reading, a good ending to a peaceful Sunday. She grabbed the note pad she kept near the phone and wrote down the letters EGBOK. "Everything's Going to Be Okay." It was something Teri's mother had told her to remember in difficult times. To Lauren, it felt like a personalized message just for her.

She reached for her bookmark on the nightstand, reasoning that that was a good message for her subconscious to repeat to her during the night. She was about to reach to turn off the light when the phone rang. She stared at the phone, willing it to be a call about someone from church who'd just had a baby and who needed dinner brought in, but she knew it was past time that anyone from church would call. Maybe it was a call from her brother a time zone away who had forgotten that it was 9:30 in Colorado instead of 8:30.

She told herself she could answer it and find out who it was or she could not answer it and worry about who it might have been. At least if she answered it, she reasoned, she had a chance of knowing for sure.

"Hello."

"Hello, Lauren." Her breath caught as she recognized the deep voice. "May I please speak to Kendall?"

"No, I'm sorry. He's, he's sleeping."

"He sure is sleeping. The big sleep. Do you really think I've been fooled all this time by your little evasions?"

"What kind of a sadistic jerk are you?"

"I'm watching you Lauren. For all you know, I'm watching you right now. Do you really think that cardboard cutout in your bedroom window is going to scare anyone away?"

She slammed the phone down, terrified, wondering what to do. *Think Lauren*. She looked at the clock. It was still early enough that she could call Bryan. He had offered to help. She had his business card downstairs. Pulling on her robe, she made her way down the hall, her mind racing. *Why didn't I leave his card in my purse instead of tacking it up? He gave me a memory trick for his number, but I'm so shook up I can't remember it. Lloyd pointed out that my latch wasn't secure, so anybody could go in the backyard. But you can see into these backyards from that little park on the hill, too. What if I'm being watched right now?* She took a deep breath. *I'm letting my imagination run wild now.*

She turned on the light at the top of the stairs but decided not to turn on any other lights. For all she knew, she was being watched even at that moment, and she didn't want to illuminate the whole house. She walked cautiously through the family room and into the kitchen. In the dim light, she saw the dark figure of a man in front of her refrigerator. She let out a bloodcurdling scream and reached for something to defend herself with, grabbing the heavy metal sharpening steel, the tallest item sticking out of the knife block. Whirling around, she brandished it menacingly at the . . . cardboard cutout of Kendall in his dress uniform. She put a hand on her chest. Her heart felt as if it were pounding hard enough to break her ribs. She laid the metal wand on the counter and doubled over, trying to get her breathing to return to normal. Frightened by her screams, Dirk appeared at the top of the stairs.

"What's the matter, Mommy?"

She took a deep breath. "Everything is okay." She repeated to herself the message from the book. *EGBOK. Everything is Going to Be Okay. Everything is not okay right now, but someday everything is going to be okay.* She hurried to the top of the stairs and gave her little boy a hug. By the time she got there, her youngest son in his Cookie Monster footie pajamas was also looking at her with wide observant eyes.

"Dirk, did you move Dress-Daddy in front of the fridge?"

"Yeah, in case he got hungry in the night," Dirk said.

"Hungwy," echoed Brett. "Monsteh."

Lauren hugged Brett, remembering that each new uttered word was a breakthrough. She hoped he was thinking more about the monster on his pajamas who wanted cookies rather than the one that had scared his mother. Children who were at an age where they needed to be protected from the monsters under the bed could benefit from having a parent who wasn't worried about what lurked in her own closet.

"Okay, from now on, please don't move the daddies around without Mommy knowing where they are, because in the dark . . ." She let out a deep sigh. "I thought there was a bad man in our house, and it scared me. I'm sorry I woke you up. Everything is okay. Everything is going to be okay."

After she tucked the boys back in bed, she retrieved Bryan's business card from her bulletin board. She moved Dress Daddy back to his recent post in the small formal living room with the bay windows. She didn't use the octagonal room much. It was perfect for visiting with one or two people who stopped by. She plopped down in one of the chairs, draping one leg over the arm. She addressed her cardboard husband. "Kendall, you wouldn't let the terrorists win, and I'm not going to let this terrorist win. I'm *not* going to be reduced to living in fear. I'm going to shine a light in every corner if I have to."

She could almost hear him. The words felt so real, she wanted to believe he really was communicating with her somehow.

"I'm not the only hero in this family."

87

Chapter Fifteen

Shining a Light

L auren dialed the number scribbled across the bottom of the business card, mentally kicking herself because she hadn't remembered the easy memory trick Bryan had given her for his number. "Hello, Bryan. This is Lauren Baylor. I had another one of those phone calls, and I remembered that you said you might be able to help me find out who's behind the calls."

She described the content of the call and he listened intently. "Okay first, do you feel safe now? Do you want me to come over and check things out?"

"I turned on the outside lights before I went back to bed and looked in the backyard. There's new snowfall and I didn't see any footprints."

"So he was probably bluffing about being able to see you right then. He didn't give any details, like saying he could see your bedroom light on or something that would make you suspect that he was truly nearby?"

"No. I appreciate your offer to come over, but . . ."

"But?"

"Having a man I barely know come over at ten o'clock at night, even a police officer, well that doesn't make me feel very safe either."

"What can I say to that? I believe trust has to be earned. I hope someday I can earn yours. If you're feeling safe for the night and don't want me to come check things out, I could come over tomorrow evening after my shift. I might be able to trace what cell tower the calls are coming from. He could be calling from a landline, too. If you had the number, we could do a reverse look-up and maybe find some information that way. Does he call at any particular time?"

"Usually around bedtime, but he's been calling more often and at different times of day lately."

"How about if I swing by early evening and we can take it from there. Do you want me to bring a Christmas movie and a pizza so that we aren't just sitting around waiting for your phone to ring or would that seem suspiciously like a date?"

She hesitated. "Can you make it a family movie?"

"Have your kids seen *The Muppet Christmas Carol*?" Bryan asked. "That's one of my favorites."

"Not this year. That's a great choice and it's one we don't have," Lauren said.

"Okay, *The Muppet Christmas Carol* it is," Bryan said. "And maybe the best thing I can do right now is try to take your mind off all this."

"That's a good idea. I was so jumpy after the call that when I went downstairs to find the card with your phone number on it, I almost gave myself a heart attack when I saw the cardboard Kendall that Dirk had moved into the kitchen."

He chuckled. "Excuse me for laughing. I'm sure it wasn't funny at the time."

"No, but I can see the humor in it now," Lauren said. "I grabbed the nearest heavy metal object, a knife sharpening steel, and was prepared to bludgeon it to pieces."

"That piece of cardboard would have been helpless against you."

"Hey, don't make fun. Don't you go to the shooting range and shoot at cardboard cutouts?"

"Yes, now that you mention it, I'm pretty awesome at offing cardboard culprits myself."

"Speaking of which, I was running bathwater for Dirk and Brett yesterday and while I was out in the hall getting towels, Dirk decided it had been a long time since his favorite cardboard Half-Daddy had a bath. Now he's inconsolable because his dad is ruined. I'm trying to dry it out, but honestly, as attached as he is to that one, I can only imagine the stares if I start showing up places with this warped, water-logged cardboard soldier propped up in the pew or the restaurant."

"Did you ever see the movie *And Then There Were None?* It sounds to me like someone is offing the cardboard dads, one at a time. First a drowning, then an assault with a deadly weapon. I think we'd better get a protective detail on the other two."

She felt much better after a few minutes on the phone with Bryan. Talking to him, she really did begin to believe E was G to B OK.

"Okay, I can probably get to sleep now that my adrenaline levels are back to normal."

"Actually elevated levels can stay in your system for the better part of the day. If you've got any heavy lifting or deep cleaning to do, tomorrow would be your day." He switched gears. "Lauren, just a hunch, but have you ever thought Lloyd might somehow be connected to these phone calls?"

"It isn't Lloyd. I'd know his voice."

Silence ensued. "Okay, I know what you're thinking. Of course I'm going to cast suspicion on the competition."

"How do you do that?" Lauren asked.

"Read minds? You learn to be observant and you learn to read people. Take for example, Lloyd's little girls. They have dark hair like Lloyd but their olive complexions could mean they have some Latin blood."

"Yes, I can see that. He has kind of a fair complexion compared to his daughters."

"Sure, that sounds better than pasty paleface, I guess. Let's say from their appearance they had definite Spanish heritage. Then I would wonder if abandoning her children sounds like something a Latin woman would do, because for the Latin women I know, their children are their lives. Then I would think about their names— Marie and Kathleen. What would you say about them?"

"They're traditional names."

"Exactly! They're old-fashioned names, showing a respect for tradition and old-fashioned values. The name Marie, as a form of Mary, shows a particular respect for religion. Biblical names, but especially that one, are, generally speaking, not given to children of parents who don't esteem religion. It could be that the parents have shared values that resulted in those names, for example, or as another option, you could have an ultra-controlling almost religious-fanatic husband imposing his will on a submissive woman when it comes to naming the children."

"That description could fit with Lloyd. It sounded like he almost spent his last dime fighting for custody of his daughters, was willing to lose his house over it, and that he didn't approve of the moral choices his ex-wife was making."

"So when he tells it, he probably makes her sound like a floozy, but it may just have been that she had dates with two different men in the same weekend. He may have convinced himself that he was rescuing his daughters from their mother by fighting so hard for custody when in reality joint custody may have been in the better interest of the girls, that even if he didn't approve of her choices, she might have been a loving mother. And Lloyd further cemented that disapproval by removing them physically. You don't quit a job at Motorola to work construction and why move from sunny Florida to chilly Colorado. So if I was looking at your friend Lloyd, as a police officer, I'd say that something doesn't add up."

"Actually he was laid off from Motorola. He was just being too macho to admit that. You were both trying a little too hard at that party."

"So maybe we were. Can you blame us? So anyway, you play with it like a puzzle, finding the pieces that fit and the pieces that don't fit. Then there are the pieces that from a distance look like they fit but when you get them up close, they have that little knob on them and no matter how hard you try, you can't get that piece into the puzzle in that spot."

"Lloyd can be manipulative, that's for sure."

"Like at the Christmas party when he sent his two little girls over to drag you back to his table just as we were being introduced?"

"You noticed that?"

"Why do you think I brought my plate over and sat by you? I mean other than the fact that I wanted to get to know you? As a police officer, you have to learn how to manipulate people, so poor Lloyd learned the hard way that you can't manipulate a manipulator."

"Thank you for not trying to manipulate me, anyway," Lauren said.

"I'm manipulating you right now."

"How?"

"Are you still thinking about that phone call?"

She laughed. "You're good. Remind me to watch out for you."

"In detective work, you have to ask these kinds of questions, over and over, turning the situation around, looking at it from different angles, kind of like solving a Rubik's Cube. And like a Rubik's Cube, one answer may change other things you thought you knew for sure. Suddenly you've got that one yellow square in the middle of the green section you thought you had completed. As with any skill, you get better over time. You have enough successes to learn to trust your instincts and enough failures to remain humble and human. The best work is done when you combine your instincts with the evidence. Instincts can be wrong but the evidence doesn't lie."

"And is part of your manipulation of me that Lloyd serves so handily as the subject of all these examples? You know, I met an old girlfriend of Kendall's that gave off some pretty hostile vibes. Maybe she's got a brother or someone calling me."

"Okay, I don't like Lloyd. You've got my number. I've made no secret of that, but he's innocent until proven guilty, and you're probably right that I can't be entirely objective about the guy. One little piece of circumstantial evidence can be nothing more than coincidence. But combined with other pieces of evidence, it can shed more light on the situation, so all I'm asking is for you to be aware. Another thing you can do is feed someone a little misinformation and watch for a flash of confusion or disbelief on their face."

"Interesting. There's something that came to mind about Lloyd when you said that, but now I can't think what it was. Wait! I remember now. For some reason, he didn't seem to want his daughter to talk about Barbie dolls and her mother. He cut her off rather obviously. I guess that's kind of stupid. What could that possibly have to do with these phone calls?"

93

"Well, there you go! Two pieces of evidence. Let's string him up." He paused. "No, that's not stupid. If you remember exactly what it was, write it down. When you're trying to follow a trail of evidence, it's like connecting the dots. There's that illuminating moment when you can finally see what the picture is supposed to be. Before that, it can all seem like random dots. I'll tell you this, Lauren, and you can judge for yourself whether I'm just being petty and jealous, but I don't have good feelings about your friend Lloyd. Just be careful."

"Bryan?"

"Yeah?"

"Thanks for being there. Thanks for taking the time to help me calm down."

"Don't mention it."

"I'm going to try and go to sleep now. Thanks again."

"Sweet dreams, Lauren."

Chapter Sixteen

A Handshake or a Kiss

When Lauren had talked with Bryan Sunday evening about coming over on Monday, it had slipped her mind during their late night conversation that Lloyd would be picking up his daughters about the same time Sergeant Everett was due to arrive. Hustling the girls out the door, she felt rude not even inviting Lloyd inside for a minute, but the last thing she needed or wanted was these two men encountering one another again. *I'm babysitting for Lloyd. Bryan is helping me with something as a friend. I don't owe either of them an explanation about anything.*

When Lloyd knocked, Lauren met him at the door with Marie and Katie, ready to go.

"You're in a hurry tonight," he commented.

"Yes, I am. Thanks for understanding." *No more explanation needed or coming.* She grabbed two little quilted coats off the coat rack near the door, where she'd hung them earlier, making sure they were easily accessible for a quick departure. "Green coat for Katie. Purple coat for Marie, right?"

"You look nice. So what are you . . .?" Lloyd began.

She cut him off and fixed him with a look. "See you tomorrow morning."

She saw Lloyd's brake lights flash bright momentarily when he passed the black truck and wondered whether he'd slowed down to get a better look. She wasn't sure he'd recognize the truck, unless he'd taken note of the vehicle Bryan had driven to the church party. She halfway expected Lloyd to turn around and come back for a missing doll or use some other lame excuse to show up back at her house, but perhaps even Lloyd knew how transparent that would look. Likewise, when Bryan rang her doorbell, she wasn't sure he'd noticed Lloyd driving away from her house. It he had, he didn't mention it.

He held out the square box. "Anyone at this address order a pizza?" He paused. "Sorry to come in uniform, but I didn't have time to go home and change. I hope it doesn't start your neighbors gossiping. I did switch vehicles at least. And I don't have my gun."

She smiled and opened the door. "As long as they don't see you escorting me out of here in handcuffs, we're good."

Around the time the Ghost of Christmas Past arrived in the movie, the phone rang, but it wasn't the mystery caller. It was Lloyd calling to let Lauren know that he would be armed with his tools and supplies when he came the following evening to pick up the girls.

"I've got everything to replace the damaged wood under your kitchen sink."

"Great! I'll see you tomorrow then."

"If I have time, I'll get the deadbolt for the garage door. And I can pick up something for dinner, if you'd like."

"We'll figure something out."

"Super! I'll see you tomorrow then."

"Bye."

Lauren hung up the phone and saw the inquiring look on Bryan's face as she turned to face him. "It wasn't the phantom."

"Yeah, I figured that."

"Just organizing some repair work I'm having done."

"That's a good idea. Is your handyman a *lowly carpenter* by any chance?" Bryan inquired.

"Is there some reason this would be considered official police business?" Lauren grabbed another slice of pizza and took a bite, rendering her temporarily unable to answer any more questions.

No more questions were asked. No more questions were answered. And no more phone calls came in that evening, mainly due to a warning call Lloyd had made to Jason.

After the movie ended, Dirk peppered Bryan with questions about everything from the siren in his car to rounding up bad guys.

"Okay guys, it's bedtime. Let's get your jammies on."

"But I have more policeman questions!" Dirk protested.

"I'm sure Officer Everett will come over again sometime, so you don't have to ask him all the questions at once." She grabbed some pajamas out of a nearby laundry basket.

"Lauren, while you're getting the boys down, do you mind if I look at the placement of the cardboard cutout in your bedroom? I was thinking that if you moved him to a different window, your caller might comment on that, and then we'd know for sure if he was watching your house on a regular basis."

"Good idea. Why don't you follow me upstairs, and you can help me figure out the best location. There's a little reading alcove off my bedroom, and I don't think you can see that window from the park. Maybe you can figure out a good placement while I get the boys down."

Lauren and Bryan met in the hall. "I followed your suggestion and put him in the alcove. I love that big chair you have in there."

"It's called a Chair-and-a-Half. There's room for an adult and a kid, or two if they're little. That's our favorite spot for bedtime stories."

They headed downstairs and to Lauren's disappointment, Bryan headed to the front door, grabbing his jacket off the back of a chair where he'd draped it when he came in. She realized with a pang of disappointment that she had been looking forward to some time alone with him.

"I've probably stayed about as long as I should. It looks like he's not going to call tonight."

"He's called late a few times and has probably figured out that I don't answer my phone after ten."

"So did this default to a date, then?"

"Family Movie Night."

"Gotcha! Okay, so I don't have to be worried about whether you're going to try and kiss me. Whew!" He wiped his brow. "There must be something acceptable somewhere between an impersonal handshake and a passionate kiss." He bowed, and reached for her hand. "It was a pleasure being in your company, m'lady." He planted a quick kiss on the back of her hand, and he was off into the night.

Lauren stood inside the door and watched him get into his truck, marveling that a kiss on the hand from Bryan had left her tingling with emotion when a kiss on the lips from Lloyd had not stirred her at all. She watched as he drove off, wishing he had stayed a little longer.

Chapter Seventeen

Playing Family

Tuesday after he got off work, Lloyd showed up with his tools, as well as a bucket of fried chicken, some doughnuts and some eggnog. After a couple of hours hard at work, he proudly showed Lauren his handiwork. He demonstrated the deadbolt that now secured the door between the garage and the house and handed her the key. The under-sink repair was also done. He had ripped out all the rotted wood and replaced it. Lauren was truly impressed with his handyman skills. Over and above the call of duty, he had also hung some Christmas lights outside the house, inspiring her to finally put the decorations on the tree. They'd turned it into kind of a party with his daughters and her little boys. She finally felt like she was getting a little of the Christmas spirit.

It didn't escape Lauren's notice that she was probably playing right into Lloyd's hands, because she was starting to become attached to Marie and Katie. She couldn't help it. The thought of the two little girls having a mother somewhere who didn't even bother to contact them over the holidays was heart wrenching.

That evening before he left, she decided to ask him about it, steering him into her small living room. Lloyd frowned when he saw the cardboard Kendall in his dress greens standing by the window. Lauren either ignored him or didn't notice the look on his face. "The girls were talking today, and I was wondering something. Has their mother sent them anything for Christmas?"

Lloyd became defensive immediately. "What did they say? What did you hear?"

"I heard Marie ask Katie if she thought their mother would send anything. It about broke my heart." She hesitated. "I know this might be different than how you would do things, but if she truly isn't going to send them anything, I'd go and buy something and wrap it and pretend it came in the mail from their mother."

Lauren's phone rang in the middle of their conversation.

"I'm not going to get it. I'm not going to give that pervert the satisfaction of knowing he has rattled me. I've decided to screen all my calls on my answering machine. I guess he's figured that out because he's been leaving messages instead of just hanging up."

"What does he say?"

"I don't really want to think about or talk about that right now, okay?" She took a deep breath. "So have you thought about getting them something and saying it's from their mother."

"I hadn't thought of doing something like that," Lloyd said. "I hate to lie to my girls."

"I'd rather be a little deceptive than to watch their hearts break."

He touched her arm. "Yeah, maybe you're right. You know what it's like, Lauren? It's as if she divorced all of us, like she just forgot that she ever had any kids in the first place." He paused. "Hey, I've got a great idea. Let's see if tomorrow night one of my nieces can come over here and watch all the kids and you and I can go Christmas shopping for them. You've probably got shopping to do for the boys, too."

Lauren considered this. *It would mean two evenings in a row spent with him, which is kind of overkill. And there's no doubt in my mind that he's successfully keeping me from having any free time to spend with anyone else. On the other hand, when you have lots of packages to carry into the house, it's kind of nice to have a man around, and all this activity is keeping me from sinking into a depression like last Christmas. I'm just going to enjoy the holidays and help Lloyd make Christmas nice for the girls and then after the New Year, I'll reestablish some firmer boundaries with him.*

"Well yeah, I do, actually, and I wanted to get something for Marie and Katie, too. I could use your input on that."

* * *

The Pearl Street Mall was crowded with holiday shoppers. Lauren didn't resist when Lloyd took her elbow and navigated her to the toy store. He picked up a gigantic Lego play set.

"Do you think the boys would like this?"

100

"That's way too big, Lloyd. I'm not even spending that much on them. And that one says it's for ages 8 and up. I don't really expect you to get my boys anything."

"But you're getting something for my girls."

"Yes, but nothing that extravagant. And I've been watching them every day. I'm kind of getting attached to them."

"Can't I get attached to your boys? You know, they need a father every bit as much as my girls need a mother. Did you know that when we were at McDonald's and you asked me to take Dirk to the bathroom, I noticed he didn't stand up and . . .'"

Her cheerfulness vanished. "I'm a single mom. I can only be a role model in so many ways. Kendall was deployed during most of his toilet training. I'm sure he'll figure it out sooner or later. Some of my friends with sons have told me not to push it, that from a housekeeping point of view, little boys don't exactly have good aim, so we didn't really worry about it."

"I'm just telling you that to show you that your boys need a father."

"I *know* that, but I'm sorry, Lloyd. I can't marry you just so you can teach my sons how to stand up and pee like a man." She pretended not to see the look of surprise and amusement on the face of the shopper who overheard that remark. "You're pushing it again, Lloyd."

"I guess I was thinking that well, you know, spending time with you after work, and with the kids getting along so well, it just started to feel like . . ."

"Yeah, I know. It feels like a family." *Except maybe the part about the kids getting along.* "I have to admit it makes me a little uncomfortable, because the reality is that we're two lonely people playing family for the holidays."

"This could become our reality, Lauren."

She held up her left hand, reminding him that she still wore her wedding rings. "We've been together nearly every night this week after you come to pick up the girls. I'm giving in because of the holidays. This can't last. You understand that, don't you?"

"Except Monday," Lloyd pointed out. "You thought you rushed me off soon enough, but I saw him pull up."

101

"Are you spying on me now, Lloyd? Not that it's any of your business, but I told you why Bryan was here. And yes, he brought in dinner and a movie for the kids. What's the difference between that and what you've been doing lately? I know. For someone who isn't dating, I'm sure having a lot of in-house dinner-and-a-movie nights. I'm just trying not to crash like I did last year. Can you understand that?"

"Well this week I'm ahead so far. I guess that'll have to be good enough." He picked up a package of plastic play food. "Okay, so what did you have in mind to get the girls?"

Lauren shook her head and sighed and decided to just let that remark pass. She turned to a display of singing hamsters and started pushing the buttons on their toes to get them all singing and dancing at once. "I was looking for some Disney stuff. The other day I came into the room and they were pretending to be a couple of Disney stars—Hannah Montana and Lizzie McGuire. I don't think Lizzie McGuire stuff is out anymore, but I think you can still find Hannah Montana movies or videos." Lauren began to poke through the movies on the shelf and didn't notice the distressed look that crossed Lloyd's face.

"Oh yeah, they used to love watching Hannah Montana. You're very observant to have picked that up. I was actually kind of relieved when it went off the air, but you can still watch it online. There's a whole website dedicated to that show. Marie was almost as obsessed with Hannah Montana as Dirk is with his cardboard dad."

"Speaking of cardboard Dad, we had a little mishap, and he had to go to rehab."

"Rehab?"

"Dirk put him in the tub, so he's drying out. I'm sorry. That was kind of a dumb joke."

"I'm glad you're getting to the point where you can joke about it," Lloyd said.

"Oh, you know. Sometimes you have a choice. You can laugh or you can cry. I had a good laugh about it with . . ." Her voice trailed off and she suddenly became very interested in a selection of stuffed animals.

"With *whom?*"

"With Bryan." *I already let it slip that he's helping me with the phantom caller.* "We were just talking on the phone." Even though Bryan had suggested that Lloyd might have something to do with the calls, and while she often found him obnoxious and pushy, she found it hard to believe he could be involved, especially as she shopped with him for toys while Christmas carols played in the background. "You know, about the calls. As a police officer, I thought he might be able to find something out."

"So what has he found out?"

"That's not what we were talking about. I was just trying to explain how we were laughing about Dirk putting the cardboard dad in the tub and how I got scared coming downstairs and thought there was someone in my kitchen because Dirk had moved one of them and put him in front of the fridge and I almost assaulted him. Anyway, Bryan made a joke about them being picked off one by one, like that movie, *And Then There Were None,* so I reminded him that he went to the shooting range, so he said something about being pretty good at offing cardboard cutouts himself."

"And you're telling me this why?"

"I don't know. I know you don't really like my cardboard Kendalls, so I thought you might be interested to know that they were being eliminated, one by one. You're always telling me I'm obsessed with them, too, not just Dirk. I guess I was just trying to show you that I could laugh about it. I thought that might be good news to you, a sign that I'm healing a little bit. I actually asked Bryan . . ." She stopped. It was almost as hard for her to say as it had been hard for her to consider doing. "I couldn't do it myself, and it was ruined, so I asked Bryan if he would get rid of the one that got ruined in the tub."

"Yes, that is good news."

"That I threw away my husband?"

"No, I mean it's good news that you're beginning to heal." He frowned. "But I don't like that guy. I don't trust him. You can't assume that all police officers are good people just because they're in law enforcement. Haven't you ever heard of a crooked cop? Just be careful."

Chapter Eighteen

A Visionary Man

After they carried the packages in and hid them in the garage, Lauren looked in on the boys, both asleep in their beds. Marie and Katie were asleep on the floor on the air mattress she had inflated, covered with one of her spare quilts. Lloyd's niece was asleep on the sofa with a throw draped over her and one pillow under her head and one over, the latest issue of *People* magazine open on the floor next to her.

Lloyd pulled Lauren aside into the little living room. "I need to talk with you before I take the girls and the babysitter home."

"This sounds serious," Lauren said. "Should I sit down?"

"It is." He paced back and forth in front of the window as she watched from the small loveseat, curling one leg underneath her and leaning back onto a throw pillow. "Ever since it happened last night, I've been praying for how I could tell you, or even if I *should* tell you. I told myself maybe it was meant just for me, like with Mary when the angels talked with her and like the scriptures say, 'she kept these things and pondered them in her heart.'"

"I'm sorry, but I'm not following you, Lloyd. Are you *pregnant?*"

He remained solemn. "This isn't a joke, Lauren."

"Then what is it?"

"I'm so sorry about how I have acted about your cardboard cutouts of your husband. He really is a kind and caring man who worries about you and the boys so very much and wants you to be happy again."

She raised an eyebrow. "Oh, you've *talked* to him?"

He hesitated for dramatic effect. "I'm not sure if you'll believe me or not, but I have."

"What?" She straightened up and leaned forward, furrowing her brow. *This is too weird, even for Lloyd.*

"It was a dream, only not a dream. I mean it wasn't jumbled and unreal like lots of dreams are or the kind where you can't remember it when you wake up. It was vivid and real and I can remember every word."

He doesn't really expect me to believe this, does he? "I'm listening." She folded her arms across her chest and leaned back into the pillow again, giving him a studied look.

"He's really worried about you and the boys, especially Brett, you know, with him not talking yet. Kendall and I were walking along the beach together."

Ah, a moonlight walk on the beach. How cliché. "What else did he say?"

"He asked me to take care of you—of you and the boys. He said I was brought here, reunited with Charlene so I would be in the right place at the right time. He told me it was his time to go, but that he was among the angels working to make sure you and the boys would be taken care of."

"Really, Lloyd? You know why I find this hard to believe? If Kendall had a chance to come visit somebody, even if it was just in a dream, I know for a certainty that he would have visited *me* and not you."

"I don't know the answer to that. I know he told me that you were his only addiction. You and March Madness. So I don't know why he would visit me and not . . ."

March Madness? How could Lloyd know about Kendall's obsession with March Madness? She stared hard at the cardboard cutout of her husband in his dress uniform, willing him to give her some sort of a sign if Lloyd was messing with her mind. Nothing happened. *If you can appear to Lloyd, appear to me right now and tell me if he's lying.* "What else?" she whispered.

"He told me how happy he was that we were together during the holidays and that if I was patient, you'd come to love me." He continued on before she had too much time to think about that. "He showed me his thumb, the scar he had from the Christmas he was putting together the tricycle for Dirk and stabbed himself in the hand with a screwdriver."

That's a memory nobody else would know about. Is it my grief for Kendall that's making me so resistant to Lloyd?

He knelt down in front of her. "I shouldn't have told you. I'm sorry. I should have known it would upset you."

Lauren began to cry. "It's all so confusing."

"It doesn't have to be. It could all be very simple, Lauren. I see now how wrong my jealousy has been. I've been so threatened by your memories of him, but we really both want the same thing—your happiness. And he wanted me to tell you that he's fine, well and whole again and that you should cease to be tormented by the manner of his death."

* * *

Lauren found it hard to fall asleep. She'd said her prayers, waiting for some calm feeling about the things that Lloyd had told her. She would have loved to hear something from Kendall, anything. But through Lloyd? Some of the things he'd said had been comforting and she wanted them to be true. All that came was a feeling that though it all *sounded* true, it still didn't *feel* right. But how had he known those things?

Eventually she drifted off to sleep, hoping that if it were all true, Kendall would make an appearance in *her* dreams. Instead she dreamt that she had moved to Kentucky to become a country western singer and partway through a performance she panicked when she remembered that she hadn't gotten a babysitter for the boys, had left them home alone in Colorado to fend for themselves. Then a girl she remembered from girls' camp when she was a teen-ager showed up and told her she would never make it in Nashville, which wasn't even in Kentucky anyway, because she had never learned how to make a fire by rubbing two sticks together. It had been a regular dream—a regular disjointed disappointing dream that didn't make any sense and didn't have Kendall in it.

In the morning she awoke with a vague memory of her talk with Lloyd the evening before and she almost wondered if she had imagined it. But when he showed up with the girls, she realized it had been all too real. The best she was able to do was tell herself that she didn't need to make any decisions about anything at the moment.

She opened the door and Katie and Marie came inside. Katie gave her a big hug. "I want you to be my new mommy." Lauren looked at Lloyd, standing on the other side of the screen door, looking as hopeful as she'd ever seen him look before.

"I'm through being jealous of Kendall, Lauren, because I know in my heart that if I can be patient, you and I are going to be together."

She looked over quickly to see if Dirk had heard that. "Okay, Lloyd. You told me what you needed to tell me. I'm thinking about it. Now is the time for you to be like Mary and keep these things and ponder them in your heart, if you get my drift."

Chapter Nineteen

It's a Wonderful Life

On Thursday when Lloyd came to pick up the girls, he had another movie in hand and a big bag of sandwiches from Arby's. "I was wondering if we could watch *It's a Wonderful Life*. It really isn't Christmas unless you watch that, is it?"

"Three nights in a row, Lloyd? Did it ever occur to you that I might have other plans?"

"Do you?"

"Well, nothing concrete, but . . ."

"Then let's get this party started!" He made himself at home and walked into the family room and spread the food out on the coffee table and inserted the DVD into the player. "I thought about taking everyone out to the movies. At least we don't have to put up with Dirk making a scene anymore because he can't take his cardboard dad to the movies."

"Lloyd, you really are a two-steps forward, three-steps-back kind of guy, aren't you? I thought you told me you had given up being jealous of the cardboard Kendalls." *You have no idea how it breaks my heart to see my son missing his dad, even if it's just his cardboard one.*

"Oh, I have. I was only thinking of the expense of having to buy an extra movie ticket. I mean you didn't get rid of it on purpose or anything, but I think it's for the better. It was time," Lloyd said.

Lauren was really starting to wish her mother wasn't in Italy. She could really use her listening ear. Although she had recently felt closer to her mother-in-law than to her mother, in part because of their shared loss, she didn't feel comfortable talking to Janet about men she was considering dating. Her mother was a down-to-earth lady, if somewhat meddlesome. Lauren remembered her first heartbreak, when her boyfriend had broken up with her and had started to date another girl. "But he kissed me!" she had protested.

"A kiss isn't a contract," her mother had said, matter-of-factly. "He's the first boy to break your heart. Probably won't be the last."

She knew her mother had been overly excited about her blind date with Lloyd, but she had to believe part of that was that it was an indication that she was coming back to life. She knew that if she laid out all the details of everything, her mother would have been able to give her good advice about all the stuff going on with Bryan and Lloyd. Cutting through the crap was her mother's specialty.

* * *

Lloyd had just taken a big bite of a French dip sandwich when the phone rang. He jumped up. "Let me get it, Lauren. If it's him, it'll show him there's a man around the house." He picked up the phone attached to the wall in the kitchen as she listened to his end of the conversation.

"No, Lauren's not available." There was a slight pause. "No, he's not available either, but I think you already know that." There was a longer pause. "Me? I'm her boyfriend, Sergeant Everett, Boulder police department. We're tracking this call as we speak." There was another pause. "Malicious mischief. Terroristic threatening. We'll throw something at you and see if it sticks. If you know what's good for you, you will cease making these phone calls. We're just a few steps behind you."

Lauren noticed a strange look on Lloyd's face as he hung up the phone.

"Why did you say you were Bryan?"

"It just came to me, that saying I was a police officer might scare him off," Lloyd explained.

"What did he say, at the end?" Lauren asked. "I saw that look on your face."

Lloyd's tone became solemn. "I don't know if I should tell you. For all I know, you'll think I'm making it up."

"Try me."

110

"No, you won't believe me, anyway. Let's just see if the calls stop."

He sat back down on the sofa and held out his arms to Lauren, hoping to comfort her, but she just shook her head and moved to the far end of the sofa, pulling the throw off the back of the sofa and wrapping herself in it protectively.

By the time George Bailey got married, all four of the kids were asleep, splayed out on the floor of the family room like a sleep-walker's version of Twister. Lloyd paused the movie while Lauren retrieved blankets from a closet in the hall and covered each of them. He watched the tenderness with which she ministered to his little girls, the same tenderness she showed to her own little boys, and he hoped that someday she would see that they belonged together.

While she covered the children, Lloyd took the opportunity to move closer on the sofa to where Lauren had been sitting. When she came back, she didn't relocate to keep her distance. It was all the encouragement he needed. He waited until a pivotal scene, when the angel told George that if he had not rescued his brother from the icy pond, his brother would not have saved the men on the transport. He knew she was thinking of Kendall, but he was willing to ride on his coattails if it meant getting closer to Lauren.

"I'm sorry about what I said earlier about Dirk and his cardboard dad. I just meant that I hoped Dirk would have accepted his father's death by now." He knew he needed to recover from his earlier blunder, and he had no idea how she was processing the telephone call, so he spread it on a little thicker, speaking softly there in the dim light. "Don't you wish Kendall could have had an angel show him how much his actions have meant in the lives of others?"

He felt her relax and lean into him. He reached around behind her and began to knead the muscles in her neck, gently moving the throw blanket out of the way. "You're tense. You carry so much responsibility on these shoulders. I wish you'd let me help you with some of the burdens."

111

Part of her wanted to resist, but another bigger part of her that night longed to be touched and loved and protected again. She closed her eyes and gave in to the physical sensation, feeling her tension drain away. When she was completely relaxed, Lloyd leaned over and gave her a small tentative kiss. When she didn't resist, he intensified the kiss, finally drawing away from her, his heart beating wildly. He looked into her eyes, trying to read what he saw there.

Lauren had known as soon as Lloyd began rubbing her neck that he was going to try and kiss her. Since their first kiss had been so disastrous and under less-than-perfect conditions, she'd told herself that she needed to let him kiss her again. This time the lights had been low, one of the feel-good-movies-of-all-time was on, and Christmas lights sparkled on the tree—and Lloyd had trimmed his nose hairs. But the needle *still* had not moved for Lauren.

She could tell by his sighs that Lloyd was in seventh heaven. He put his arm around her shoulder and held her tight. Too tight. Possessively tight. He whispered something in her ear about being together, but all she could hear were her mother's words ringing in her ears. *A kiss is not a contract.*

Chapter Twenty

Dueling Santas

Bryan lifted the large cardboard box out of the back of his truck. He placed the red and green luminaries along either side of the walk. It paid to have a sister who knew her way around the craft store. He set the little tea candles inside the holders and pulled a barbecue lighter from his pocket. Once the walkway to her house was festively lit, he rang the doorbell.

"Ho ho ho, Merry Christmas."

Lauren opened the door. "Santa!" It was amazing the difference an introduction and a little time spent together could make. "Are those luminaries? I love it!"

"I remembered you mentioning you liked the ones from the Christmas party," Bryan said.

He heard footsteps behind him on the walk and turned to see another Santa on approach, one who had run into heavy traffic after work. Lloyd's well-laid plan was unraveling like an old sweater. The other Santa scowled. "Those are from *you?*"

Immediately Bryan recognized his voice. *This is unbelievable.* "What are *you* doing here?"

"The same thing as you, apparently."

"Well, I was here first."

"Here on the porch maybe. I was around long before she even knew who you were."

"And your Santa suit looks like it has been around way longer than either of us. Where'd you get that moth-eaten mess? You're a disgrace to Santas everywhere."

Lauren stood in the open doorway not quite sure how to handle this dilemma. Behind her the eyes of two little boys grew large. *Two Santas!*

"I believe Lauren was expecting me," Bryan hissed under his breath. "Beat it, you cheap imposter. I ought to arrest you for *Lloyd-ering.*"

"I have just as much right to be here as you do. And I've got Matchbox cars. Do *you* have Matchbox cars? Dirk loves Matchbox cars," Lloyd said.

"I've got Hungry Hungry Hippos, loved by generations of children. A true classic," Bryan countered.

"Yeah, well, I've got catnip and cat toys and cat food. Fancy Feast."

"Lauren has a cat?" Bryan asked.

"Ha! Three of them, actually. How well can you know the woman if you don't even know her beloved pets?"

"I have homemade divinity. Lauren says my sister's divinity is to die for," Bryan said.

"That *could* be arranged," Lloyd countered.

"Oh yeah?" Bryan puffed out his chest. "Give it your best shot. My guess is you won't even make it past my stuffing. Oh, that's right. You don't know about stuffing because you didn't *need* any."

The porch light went on and off. The two Santas stopped bickering momentarily and turned to look into the angry eyes of the object of their affections. "All right, that's it! I've had it with *both* of you. I'm not letting either one of you in."

Lauren's nerves were on edge. There had been several disturbing messages on her answering machine from the phantom caller, and she was in no mood to put up with more posturing between Bryan and Lloyd.

"If you'd stop fighting for a minute about which of you is the Alpha Santa and who has the coolest stuff or the shiniest boots, you might notice that you're totally messing up a couple of little kids who happen to believe in the jolly fat guy in the red suit. And I don't believe in either of you anymore! So take it back to the North Pole and fight it out there while I go inside and do damage control with my boys."

She slammed the door and left the two squabbling Santas on her front porch.

"Now look what *you've* done," Lloyd said.

"What *I've* done? You know, Lloyd, she isn't going to fall in love with you no matter how you stack the deck. You think because I've got a Santa suit, you can get one, too, and trot on over here and try to one-up me? You trimmed those nose hairs for nothing, buddy. Do you really think she's not going to see through you? Your motives are as threadbare as your Santa suit. And another thing, that's the lamest Santa beard I've ever seen, and I've seen some lame beards in my time." As a parting shot, Bryan reached up and yanked on Lloyd's beard and let it snap back in his face.

"Ouch!" Lloyd lunged at Bryan. He quickly stepped to the side and watched with a little too much enjoyment as Lloyd face-planted in a bank of snow. The seething Santa sat up and wiped himself off, watching as Bryan tossed his bag of toys into the back of his truck for the second time that month and sped away. All Lloyd had to show for his efforts was a small handful of fur he'd yanked from the cuff of one sleeve of Bryan's Santa suit as he went down.

Lloyd stood up, brushing himself off, shivering. The worn Santa suit wasn't much for warmth. He looked around to make sure no one was watching out the window, relatively certain that Lauren had probably hustled her little boys upstairs lest they be treated to any more aberrant behavior by the dueling Santas. He reached into his pocket and bent over, dropping the loaded cell phone into one of the luminaries lining the walk, snuffing out the small candle in the process. If all went according to plan, she would be out soon to blow out the rest of the candles and she'd discover that *someone* had dropped a cell phone while he was setting up the luminaries. From there all she had to do was follow the carefully laid clues.

"Let's see who has the last laugh now, Sergeant Everett."

Chapter Twenty-One

Take Two

Bryan stormed into his sister's house without even waiting for her to answer the door. He carried the green burlap bag, still full of toys and gifts, on his back.

"Not again? What went wrong this time?"

"Lloyd! The guy must have had some intel on when I was coming over, because he showed up with his own Santa suit, if you could call it that, and bag of toys. We kind of got into it there on the porch and Lauren ended up, probably rightly so, telling us both to get lost."

"You mean after all this you *still* haven't delivered the toys and presents?"

He pulled out one of the chairs and sat down at the kitchen table, pulling off his Santa cap and tossing it on the table. "That's what I mean. I set up the luminaries and she was just admiring them and then my worst nightmare showed up."

"She liked the luminaries, then?"

"She loved them. Thanks for helping me with that. I'm sorry I haven't come through for you. I'm sorry I haven't come through for Dad. He was such a great Santa. I'm sorry I haven't come through for *me*. A few blocks away there's a beautiful woman I think I could really fall for and I can barely get past the front door."

"You said you were over there on Monday."

"Yes, and I made a judgment call whether to try and stick around after she'd put the boys to bed, even though I could tell she wanted me to. I wanted to. You don't know how much I wanted to, but I thought it would be best if I showed I could respect her boundaries."

"I'm sure she appreciated that," Samantha said.

"Really? Because I'm not sure of anything anymore."

* * *

Lauren decided to get up early Sunday morning. She rose while the boys were still asleep and heated up the griddle to make some pancakes. She mixed up the batter and let it sit. She headed out to the garage, feeling an added measure of security as she turned the handle and released the heavy-duty deadbolt. She lifted the garage door about a foot so her feline friends could have access to food and a little more warmth than was afforded them outdoors, remembering that Lloyd had talked of installing a cat door in the side door into the garage.

"Here kitty, kitty, kitty." Gollum peaked out at her from underneath her car. *I suppose I should ask Lloyd to replace the garage door opener, so it's easier for me to park in the garage when it's so cold outside. Now I'm going to have to scrape the windows again.* Lauren poured the food into the bowl and went back inside the house, knowing the cats would feel free to feed once she was no longer around. She sprinkled some cold water on the griddle to see if it danced, a sign that it was ready.

She cooked the pancakes, putting them in a glass dish and warming them in the oven on low heat until the boys woke up. She was not inclined to wake them up any earlier than necessary. She was relishing having just a few minutes alone. She picked up a book and headed to the sofa and then she remembered the cell phone she had found the evening before when she had blown out the luminaries. She knew that one or the other of the Santas would be by once he realized it was missing. She supposed she should have opened it and checked to see if she could figure out which one of them it belonged to, but she realized she was still annoyed enough at both of them that she didn't really care.

When her own cell phone rang, she accidentally grabbed the silver phone off the end table. Looking at it for the first time, she realized it was a cheap disposable model. She flipped it open, as her own phone stopped ringing. The functions were quite simple to figure out compared to the complex phones that everyone now used. She pulled up the log of calls made, thinking she might see a list of contacts, numbers she might recognize, like Charlene's or Samantha's, something that would give her a clue whose phone it was. What she saw sent a chill down her spine. Her number came up, several times in a row. When she pushed the option for more information, she realized that the most recent calls had been made at the times she had remembered receiving calls from the mystery caller, calls that she had let go to the answering machine.

The implication was clear. Either Bryan or Lloyd had something to do with the man who had been terrorizing her over the phone. She continued to scroll down and then her heart stopped as she saw a number she recognized even though she had only called it a few times. It ended in 007, like James Bond. *Why would the person who's been calling me call Bryan?*

As if on cue, Lloyd Owens rang her doorbell. At the sight of the phone in her hand and the stricken look on her face, he knew he had struck pay dirt. Wordlessly she opened the door and he came in.

"What are you doing here, Lloyd?" *This is the second Sunday morning in a row that you've popped by.*

"I tried to call but you didn't answer. I just came by to apologize for how badly I acted last night and . . ." He stopped. "Is something wrong, Lauren? You look upset."

She held up the phone.

"You got a new phone? It doesn't look very . . ."

"I found it, last night, in one of the luminaries. I thought it might belong to you or Bryan." Her voice was flat. "I guess it wasn't you." She showed him the numbers on the phone.

"It all makes sense now, what the caller said to me the other day," Lloyd said.

"You mean the thing you didn't want to tell me?"

"I honestly didn't think you'd believe me, but maybe you will now." Lloyd dropped his voice to a whisper. "He said, 'Is she buying it, Bry?'"

He followed her over to the dining room table, taking off his jacket and hanging it over the back of the nearest chair. She pulled out the chair on the end and sat down. He took the seat next to her. Lloyd was at his smoothest when he was consoling her. "All I can think is that he was in cahoots with the caller and that the caller was reporting in to him on your state of mind after the call. Maybe that's how he magically showed up to console you after the calls.

Someone was tipping him off. It's the oldest trick in the book, pretending to help someone to throw them off the trail. Police officers and fire fighters will tell you that the person who did it is often an onlooker in the crowd."

She still couldn't get her head around it. *Bryan showed up because I called him. You're the one who showed up at all the right times after the calls.* Was it really true that the evidence didn't lie? Didn't it ever tell just a little white lie? She realized that with all her heart and soul she wanted the evidence to be lying.

Chapter Twenty-Two

Deck the Halls

She closed the phone and set it in the middle of the table. "What are you going to do?" Lloyd asked. "Are you going to call the police?"

"I don't know what I'm going to do. How do you call the police on the police?" She sighed, weary to the bones of this intrigue. "Maybe next time the guy calls I'll just tell him the gig is up. That's all I want, for the calls to stop."

She heard some stirring from upstairs, an indication that the boys were getting up. "I'd rather not discuss any of this further in front of my sons. There's been way too much commotion and upset in our lives lately. If one more thing happens, I think it's going to push me over the edge." She opened the oven door and took out the warm pancakes.

"I should let you go," Lloyd said. "I'll see you at church."

"I'm not going to church today. I made these pancakes for the boys, and as soon as they come down, I'm going to feed them and then I'm going to take them to see the two o'clock showing of one of the new Christmas movies at the fourplex."

"You're not going to church?"

"That's right, Lloyd. I'm ditching on church. I just can't do it today. I don't want to have to get dressed up, and I don't want to have to get the boys dressed up, and I don't want anybody asking me how I am. If God can forgive me for skipping out on church one Sunday, maybe I can forgive Him for letting my husband die."

"You seem pretty upset. I know this information about the phone calls has got to come as a shock. Someone you thought you could trust has . . ."

He stood up and moved behind her chair. "You're tense. I'm sure that a nice neck rub would help."

She turned and put up both her hands palms forward. "Hands off, Lloyd."

"You seemed to like it well enough the other night."

She softened. She wasn't being fair to him. He went about things awkwardly, but he was generally well meaning. "I'm messed up right now, all right? Sure, the phone thing is part of it." She faced him. "My husband was blown apart. How long do you think it takes to recover from something like that? I just can't put on my happy church face today and pretend that everything is okay and that I believe everything happens for a higher purpose." She began to cry. "He was the love of my life, and honestly, I'm not sure most days if have the capacity to ever love someone else again, not the way I love him. Love. Present tense. Not *loved*. Because I will always love him."

He frowned, looking this time at the cutout of Kendall by the door to the patio in jeans and a Colorado Buffaloes t-shirt and baseball cap. Lloyd could see his red hair in this one and was struck by how much Dirk resembled his father. Even if she eventually got rid of the cardboard Kendalls, she still had a pint-sized replica of him.

He reached for his jacket hanging over the nearby chair. "I can tell you need a day out with your boys. I'm sorry to have bothered you. I just wanted to apologize again for how I acted last night."

"Apology accepted," she said wearily. "I'm sorry, Lloyd. I really am. I'm running on empty, and there isn't a gas station in sight."

"What movie theater are you going to? The one by the high school?"

No, I'm going to drive to Denver. "Of course the close one."

* * *

Lauren felt better after watching the movie. It had been silly, but hearing her little boys' laughter and seeing their enjoyment had renewed some of her holiday spirit. She wished she hadn't had the large soda with the popcorn. She stood in front of the ladies' room. *Dirk is getting a little bit old to go into the ladies' room with me, but he's too young to send into the men's room alone. If I take them both into the stall with me, it gets awfully crowded. If I take Brett in with me, and leave Dirk waiting outside the stall I could have a repeat of that time Dirk asked a lady if she would buy him a*

122

lollipop from the tampon machine. What do other single parents do? Does anybody ever think about this? Where is the family restroom when you need it?

She looked up and saw the answer to her dilemma. She was surprised to see Lloyd headed in her direction. He had just come out of a nearby theater carrying half a container of popcorn.

He looked sheepish. "I thought your idea of going to the movie sounded good. I don't usually go to the movies on Sunday myself, but the girls were invited to a birthday party today for a girl whose mother is trying to make sure her daughter's birthday doesn't get swallowed up in Christmas. I told them they couldn't go, because we had to go to church, but then I decided maybe I am a little too inflexible about things like that, so I dropped them off at the party. Then I decided to trying to catch up to you, but driving here I realized that I've imposed on you way too much lately, so I went to that new James Bond movie."

She began with an apology, touching his arm. "I'm sorry I unloaded on you with both barrels today. And that I've been an unrighteous influence on you, getting you to ditch on church, too."

"It's okay. I get that sometimes when your trials overwhelm you, it's hard not to let it damage your faith, even temporarily."

"I'm wondering if I can impose on *you* for something."

"Sure. What can I do?"

"Would you mind taking Dirk to the restroom?" *Please just no commentary on his failure to pee like a man.*

Lloyd puffed up like he had just been awarded the Nobel Peace Prize. "I'd be glad to."

"Great! We'll meet you back here in a few minutes." She took Brett into the ladies' room. There were times she was grateful for his limited vocabulary, and this was one of them.

* * *

"Ice cream, anyone? My treat." Based on the reactions of the boys, Lauren knew she had no choice but to accept. Lloyd was a master manipulator when it came to things like that. Still, she had to admit that a couple of scoops of ice cream with some decadent toppings didn't sound half bad, and there was an ice cream parlor just across the parking lot.

Lloyd ended up finishing the rest of Brett's ice cream sundae, but Dirk polished off all of his. Lauren wiped his face the best she could with the dry napkins. "Here, let me help." Lloyd took a stack of napkins to the nearby drinking fountain and came back with a more effective cleaning method. "Hey, look, Lauren! There's a boy underneath this chocolate!"

Lauren was starting to like him again. He was a most confusing man. "So, where are you parked? I think I ought to follow you home. There's been quite a storm that kicked up while we were at the movies."

"Yeah, this isn't exactly what I'd call an ice cream sort of day. You don't need to follow me home, Lloyd. I think I can drive two miles in a snowstorm without incident."

Kendall had always treated her as a competent equal partner. She sometimes felt like Lloyd treated her like she was weak and helpless and . . . blond.

"Still, it will make me feel better. This is the kind of weather where it's so easy to go into a skid."

She sighed. "Okay, you can follow me home if it will make you feel better, but I know how to steer out of a skid. I'm not the one who just moved here from Florida."

She got out of the car and stomped through the snow and opened the garage door the rest of the way, remembering that she was going to ask Lloyd if fixing an automatic garage door was in his handyman repertoire. Now that she had the new lock on the door into the house, she hadn't worried about leaving the door open a few inches while she was at the movies so the stray cats could get in out of the cold. Luke had once joked with her and told her she had a woman's garage. There wasn't all that much stored in her garage, it was true. She had given most of Kendall's tools away to her brother, and she had someone who mowed her lawn during the summer, so she had no need of a lawn mower and lots of yard tools. The rake looked pretty lonely there in the corner with only a push broom for company.

She took note that most of the cat food was gone. She pulled the car into the garage and got the boys out of their car seats. She waved to Lloyd to send him on his way, but instead he parked his car in front of her house and followed her into the garage.

"I'm sorry, Lauren. I told you I was going to put a cat door in here for you, and I haven't done it yet. And I didn't even think about how you still have to open your garage door manually. Do you have a ladder so I can take a look at your automatic door opener and see if I can figure out what's the matter? No use replacing the whole thing if a minor tweak can fix things. It might just need battery replacement for all we know."

She left Lloyd tinkering in the garage and took the boys into the house. She took off their coats and boots, wondering about her chances of getting them to both go down for a nap. But she'd bought them candy at the movies, and she didn't imagine they'd go down easily. She grabbed the remote control and soon they were happily entertained by a cartoon show. She headed upstairs, wishing she dared lie down for a few minutes. She opened the door to her bedroom and let out a terrified scream.

Hanging by a necktie from the ceiling fan, the cardboard Kendall in the camouflage outfit dangled over her bed. She jumped up on the bed, pulling on the necktie until the whole thing came loose and fell to the bed. There was a gash of red on the bent neck, meant to look like blood. She didn't notice the little ball of fluff tangled in the tie. All she could think of was getting it down before her sons were subjected to the sight of their "bleeding" father hanging from the ceiling.

Turning, she blanched as she saw the words written on the mirror in her bathroom with a lipstick, still on the counter. **"And then there were none."** If she'd looked closer she would have seen that it was a brand-new *Cranberry Crush* lipstick from Tara Leigh Cosmetics, not one of her shades.

Lloyd rushed inside when he heard Lauren scream. She ran downstairs and grabbed the phone, dialing 9-1-1. "Someone's been in our house. They might still be here." She switched the television off as she gave her address and information to the dispatcher. Dirk and Brett watched quietly, knowing something was wrong. Brett began to whimper.

"What's the matter? Is there a window broken?" Lloyd asked.

"No, but someone's been in here. You can find out all about it when the police get here. I'd rather not subject my boys to a description. Please get the boys' coats and help me take them outside. We're not coming back in here until the police have searched every inch of this house."

She shepherded the boys outside, neglecting to get her own coat out of the hall closet. "Has your bedroom been trashed or something? I don't see anything out of sorts down here," Lloyd said. "I guess this is what happens when you ditch on church."

She fixed him with a cold stare. "Tell me you didn't just say that, Lloyd. If God worked that way, we'd all have been struck by lightning several times by now." She shivered. "Yes, it was my bedroom. It was in my bedroom. They must have come in while we were at the movies."

"I hope you didn't touch anything," Lloyd said.

She stopped short. There wasn't anything she could do to change what she'd already done. She realized that since it didn't appear anything else in the room had been touched, she would look like a hysterical nut job to the police, who would find a cardboard cutout and a necktie on her bed and would have to take her word for the terrifying scene she had encountered.

She found herself hoping that Bryan would be one of the responding officers, then reminded herself of the incriminating evidence she had found on the refillable phone. *I'm really losing it this time. I'm going nuts. There are only two men who could be behind this. And one of them is here with me.*

Lloyd looked at her shivering in the driveway and went back inside and came out with her coat.

"Thanks. I didn't even realize I was cold."

He put his arms around her, and she let him. "You're shivering. It's okay, Lauren. I'm here. Whatever it is, we'll get to the bottom of it, together."

Soon a police car pulled up in front of the house. Two uniformed officers got out, neither of them known to Lauren.

126

"Lloyd, would you take the boys over to my next-door-neighbor's house? Her name is Marilyn. See if she'd be willing to watch them for a few minutes so they don't think yellow crime scene tape is part of our Christmas decorations."

"I think they only use that if there's like, a murder."

"Then get going or there will be," she threatened.

Lloyd headed to the neighbor's house with the boys while Lauren let the officers into the house, explaining what she had seen and apologizing for contaminating the crime scene, leading them up to the bedroom. They went through every room in her house to make sure the intruder was not still in the house and searched for signs of forced entry. The officers dusted for fingerprints. They bagged what evidence they could find—a red lipstick and a piece of white fluff that and the tie.

Officer Wilmott spoke to Lauren. "There isn't any sign of forced entry. We've got a few pieces of evidence. We dusted the cardboard soldier for prints, so it isn't necessary for us to take it into evidence."

"Aren't there tests you can do at the crime lab?"

"Ma'am with all due respect, real life police work isn't quite the way they show it on television crime shows. We have to justify the expense and necessity of everything we ask for. Not to downplay your pain, but the victim was . . . cardboard."

Officer Johnston spoke. "Who else has keys to your house, Mrs. Baylor?"

"My mother-in-law has a set, in case I lock myself out."

"Anybody else?"

"Nobody else."

"You don't have a housekeeper or a pest control service or someone you gave a set of keys to once to come over and water your house plants?"

"I keep an extra set of keys in my car glove box."

She went outside with one of the officers to make sure the extra keys were still in her car. Unlocking and opening the car, she discovered the extra set of keys exactly where she had expected to find them. "I was at the movies with my car, so no one could have used these keys. And I always lock my car."

127

Lloyd had returned from the neighbor's house. One of the officers took Lloyd aside and took his statement. Lauren halfway listened to his account of running into her at the movies and following her home in the storm, tuning out what seemed like routine information. He hadn't even seen what had been staged for her in the bedroom. She felt the officers were treating her with respect, but she wondered secretly if they were going to take this case at all seriously. How did she know they were not going to go back to the precinct and make jokes about some woman calling the police because there was a cardboard man and a necktie on her bed?

Lloyd lowered his voice. "I know he's one of your own, but my conscience won't let me rest until I tell you a few things Sergeant Bryan Everett said recently to Mrs. Baylor." Lloyd recounted the conversation Lauren had told him about to the best of his recollection. ". . . and then he said he was skilled at offing cardboard culprits. He's been extremely jealous of my friendship with Lauren, Mrs. Baylor, and I suspect from the things he said, he's pretty intimidated by her *ex,* um, late husband's status as a hero."

"Since this is hearsay, we'll need to get this statement directly from Mrs. Baylor," Officer Johnston said.

The officer motioned to Lauren. "Mrs. Baylor, in light of your friend's statement, we have a few more questions we'd like to ask you."

Chapter Twenty-Three

Suspecting Santa

B ryan opened the door to his apartment to see two of his fellow officers. "Hey, what's up?"

Officer Wilmott was almost apologetic. "We're here on official business, Everett. We're investigating a break-in at the home of Lauren Baylor."

"Lauren? Is she okay? When did this happen? How did I miss it on the scanner? I didn't know you knew about our friendship. Thanks for coming by to let me know." *I need to get over there and make sure she's okay, but she hasn't been returning my calls lately. And the one time I did get through, she was very short with me. I've driven by her house a couple of times, but his car has been there every evening I've checked.*

Officer Wilmott glanced at his partner, Officer Johnston. "As you know, we have to investigate all leads, Everett. We have a few questions we need to ask you."

"Me? Don't tell me I'm a suspect."

"Based on statements from Mrs. Baylor and a Mr. Lloyd Owens, we do have a few questions."

"*Owens?* What was he doing there?"

"He was with Mrs. Baylor when she discovered the break-in," Officer Wilmott explained. "Someone hung a cardboard soldier from the ceiling fan and scrawled a threatening message on her mirror in the bathroom."

"That's awful! I have nothing to hide. I'll answer all your questions. It'll give the real culprit time to get away or cover his tracks."

Wilmott responded. "Then let's get it over with and give you a chance to show us why you *weren't* involved, so we can cross you off the list."

Bryan backed down. "Sorry. I know you're just doing your job."

Bryan answered all the questions, detailing his association with Lauren, his whereabouts during the time period in question, the reasons his fingerprints were in her home.

"So your alibi is that you were at the mall. Do you have any proof of that, any receipts? Did you buy anything, see anyone you know who could vouch for your whereabouts?"

"No and no. Wait, I bought a corndog and a soda."

"Do you have your receipt?" asked Officer Wilmott.

"Nah, told them I didn't need one. Look, I didn't hang cardboard Kendall from a ceiling fan. If you want my opinion, which I realize you don't, the guy you need to be looking at is Lloyd Owens."

"Her boyfriend?"

Bryan exploded. "He *isn't* her boyfriend!"

"He has an alibi. He was with Mrs. Baylor at the same movie theater when the intrusion occurred. He had his ticket stub. He followed her home."

"Yeah, like a stray dog. And he's been hanging around ever since. You say he was at the same movie theater. What, were they on a date?"

Officer Johnston decided to let that question go unanswered. "His fingerprints were all over downstairs but we didn't find any in the bedroom."

"Yes!" Bryan made a fist of triumph.

"We didn't find *his* fingerprints on the cardboard cutout. We found yours."

"So whoever it was used gloves. If it wasn't him, he's working with somebody. I gave you the explanation for my fingerprints."

Johnston smirked. "Yeah, I get it, Everett. You were in her bedroom and you moved the cardboard replica of her dead husband to another window. Gotcha! I don't blame you."

Bryan scowled. "It's not like that, you idiot! It's complicated. You see, Lauren's been receiving these phone calls and . . ."

"We know about the phone calls. Mr. Owens showed us a phone that was also found on the premises, a disposable cell phone. Sorry to say Everett but that phone also appears to incriminate you. There are calls made to Mrs. Baylor's home and cell phones and calls made to you on that same phone. Mr. Owens implied that you've been terrorizing the woman."

"*What?* No wonder she won't talk to me. Maybe my number *is* in the phone. I've been getting lots of strange calls lately on what up-to-now was a private cell phone. What else did that clown say about me?"

"Don't worry. We're still checking on the phone, when the calls were made, when it was activated. The truth will out. Owens says that you're jealous of the cardboard replicas, that you told Lauren she'd better get a protective detail on the other two, that you were great at offing cardboard suspects. Mrs. Baylor corroborated his statement."

"*Seriously?* She knew I was joking when I said that. Somewhere along the way she must have mentioned that conversation to Lloyd. I have no idea why she would do that, but whatever he's telling you about me, turn it around and assume he's talking about himself, and you've got your man, Dudley Do-Right. I hope you can see I'm being framed. This is amateur hour at its best. At the moment, I'd like an opportunity to face my accuser."

"I'll bet you would, Sergeant Everett. Calm down. We don't want to be bringing you up on murder charges, but if you call me Dudley Do-Right one more time, all bets are off. We're just trying to follow procedure here. Answer the rest of our questions, and then we'll let you tell your side of the story. We don't have any other leads to follow. We can't devote much more manpower to this case. After all, the victim was cardboard, and though the message on the mirror could be taken as a terroristic threat, it would appear the threat was intended for the other cardboard cutouts. We have *real* crimes to solve."

"I just need to need to know that Lauren and the boys are safe."

"I believe she said something about spending the night with her in-laws," Officer Johnston said, "But you didn't hear that here. Another thing Owens told us is that your sister sells Tara Leigh Cosmetics."

"What does Sami's cosmetic sales business have to do with this?"

"The lipstick, it said *Cranberry Crush* on it, was from that company."

"And let me guess who shared that piece of information with you. Did he tell you that his sister is one of her biggest customers?" He bit his lower lip in frustration. "I'm just wondering what it will take before Lauren kicks his sorry butt to the curb."

Wilmot reached into his pocket and pulled out a piece of white fur. "I doubt any judge in his right mind would give us probable cause and sign off on a search warrant based on this piece of evidence, considering the nature of the crime, so I'm just going to ask. Mrs. Baylor and Mr. Owens both said you're in possession of a Santa suit. Do you mind if we take a look at it? This was found on the bed at the crime scene, tangled in the tie used to hang the victim."

Bryan took a closer look at the piece of white fuzz. "Sure, I'll show you exactly where it came from, Officer, which should be the last nail in my coffin. I will willingly incriminate myself, because I'm innocent, and I trust in my ability, somehow, to prove that, with your capable assistance." He opened the hall coat closet and pulled out his Santa suit. "This could explain a lot, because if you're going to pin this crime on Santa, this proves that I've been impersonating the jolly fat guy in the red suit. Since there wasn't any forced entry, it *must* have been Santa coming down the chimney."

Bryan laid the Santa suit on his small dining room table. "So how does this work? It is like when we input a chip of paint and it tells you what make and model of car it's from? Think about how I've saved you from having to track down all the Santa suits in the greater Denver area based on this little piece of fluff. It's a Christmas miracle! It would have taken some awesome detective work to track this one down, especially considering it was my late father who purchased the Santa suit a couple of decades ago. But I'm sure I've got the receipt around here somewhere." He smacked himself in the forehead with his hand. "Damn! It's with my corndog receipt!"

"Mrs. Baylor told us you've visited her house twice in your Santa suit," said Officer Wilmott.

"So *Lauren* fingered me? Did she remember to mention that Mr. Lloyd Owens also possesses a Santa suit, because the fluff is coming off his suit a lot easier than it is off mine. So I supposedly had motive and opportunity because I find the woman attractive and because I was in her house, once? That's about as lame as it gets."

"Everett, calm down. Everything else she said about you was good. She said you'd never exhibited signs of jealousy, of the cardboard soldiers, and even when she confirmed what you said about offing the cardboard guys, she was just confirming that you said it. She wasn't the one who took it out of context. Give us a chance to do our jobs."

"That piece of fluff is definitive evidence, at least in my mind, if not in yours, that I'm being framed by Owens. That pious prig ripped that piece of fur off my suit when we got into, um, a little scuffle, on Lauren's porch when we both showed up playing Santa on the same night. He obviously planted it at the scene. Otherwise how did it get there? You can check and see that I don't have any defensive wounds from the cardboard soldier trying to fight me off. *He* didn't pluck this piece of fur off my Santa suit."

"Everett, we have to follow the chain of evidence, however contrived it appears to be," Officer Wilmott said. "The truth will out."

"As Santa, I've never made it past Lauren's front door. If you don't believe me, ask her little boy, Dirk, who is still waiting for Santa to deliver the toys and let his new cat out of the bag. One of the things you should check for is stray nasal hairs. When a nostril gets too overgrown, those things just fall out from overcrowding. On television, a hair is often the key to solving a case. I'm pretty sure Lloyd Owens must have left a trail of nasal hairs."

"Very funny, Everett," Officer Johnston said. "You know, you're right, though. I've noticed on the crime scene shows that they never have something disgusting like that, like toenail clippings or something, that help solve the crime."

"Sure. We'll keep our eyes peeled for nose hairs. Besides fingerprints and the lipstick, which was wiped clean, this piece of fur is the only piece of evidence we've got," Officer Wilmott said.

133

"Perhaps you can sniff the pits of my Santa jacket to see if I perspired in it recently. Or if you're not up to it, maybe you could call in a canine unit. If I did this, why would I have been wearing a Santa suit? So as not to attract any undue attention to myself? Did anybody report seeing a strange Santa lurking about the home? Did any neighborhood kids report running across the street with a last-minute correction to their wish list?"

"No neighbors reported anything out of the ordinary."

Bryan pointed to the sleeve of his Santa suit. "There's the bald spot. I'm sure you'll find it's a perfect match for your little bit of Santa fur. I'd show you, but I don't want to contaminate the evidence." He put his arms out in front of him. "Slap on the cuffs."

"We're going to need to take this into evidence," Wilmott said apologetically.

"I need it back by Christmas Eve."

"Sure, *Santa.*"

"Seriously, I do. I'm helping a kid from church with his Eagle Scout project. My sister loves to volunteer me for these things, always thinks that if I hang around with the church people enough, it's going to rub off on me. He collected toys for the children's hospital, and I'm the delivery guy. But if you want to be the Grinch who stole Christmas from the sick kids . . ."

"I'll see what I can do, Everett, but I make no promises."

"Owens has done a lot of handyman work for Lauren lately. He could have left a window unlatched or any of a number of other things to prevent there from being a forced entry."

"Funny you should mention it. He suggested the same thing about you, that you could have left the patio door unlatched on your visit."

"Again, if I could, he could," Bryan said. "Tell me this, which of us had been in her home most recently? More, period? He thinks he can engineer this whole thing, that nobody will do any critical thinking, that they'll just gobble up the trail of breadcrumbs like a mindless turkey being led to the slaughter. The man is an engineer, after all. They're not known for their people skills, because they think people work like machines, that you can program them and then just push the button. He worked at Motorola. Or so he said. I

134

recently discovered that Motorola closed their Boynton Beach office in south Florida in 2004. I never thought he was tan enough to have come here directly from Florida. Even an office worker has to walk to and from his car every day. I wonder what he's really been doing since then."

"That isn't our problem, Everett," Officer Wilmott said, "but you know, it would help if you had some sort of believable alibi."

"I'll get right on that."

Chapter Twenty-Four

Innocent Until Proven Guilty

S amantha opened the door and found her distraught brother on her porch. "What's going on, Bryan? I heard that someone broke in to Lauren's house. Are you working the case?"

"No, but it's in good hands with Wilmott and Johnston. I can't work the case."

"Because of your friendship with Lauren?"

"No, because at the moment I'm one of the suspects. And no, someone didn't *break* in. There wasn't any forcible entry and nobody has figured out why yet. It's a home intrusion, which, if you ask me, is what she should charge Lloyd Owens with every time he shows up unannounced on her doorstep. You know those cardboard cutouts Lauren has of her military husband—I'm sure you've at least seen the one Dirk used to take everywhere—well one of them, the one she keeps in her bedroom, was hanging by a necktie from her ceiling fan when she came home. She freaked out, as you can imagine and took it down, thinking only about not letting her boys see it. So she contaminated whatever evidence there might have been. And there was a disturbing message written on her mirror, with lipstick—with a TLC lipstick."

"Oh, my goodness! Who would be so cruel?" Then she turned her attention to a matter of greater concern. "One of *our* lipsticks was used in a crime?"

"Yes, and this might seem like a small thing, but don't you have record of all the products that people order? Charlene might be missing a lipstick."

Sami's face fell. "Oh, checking to see if Charlene is missing a lipstick would be like checking to see if Karl was missing a screwdriver. He must have sixty of them if he has one."

"Let's start by finding out if she had that shade in the first place," Bryan suggested.

"I keep everybody's history in my computer. I have a profile for each customer, and a history of their orders, you know for refills and . . ."

Bryan spoke slowly, trying to remain calm. "Enough with the sales pitch, Sami. I'm not going to sign up to be in your downline. This is just between us. The officers told me things they probably shouldn't have and now I'm telling you things I shouldn't. I'm trying to find out if this *Cranberry Crush* was one of Lauren's lipsticks that he grabbed out of her drawer or if the guy brought the lipstick with him that he used to scrawl on the mirror. Can you look that up for me, off the record?"

"Sure, I can look it up, but I can tell you right now. Lauren's a spring. I'd never recommend such a dark shade for her. Now Charlene, she's a winter. With her dark hair and olive complexion, she can pull off a true red like *Cranberry Crush*. Even if Lauren wanted to be bold, she'd want something from the maroon family, something with a touch more . . ."

Bryan picked up her bejeweled pink laptop computer from the nearby desk and carried it over to her. "The computer, Sami. I need to know who *ordered* it. Not whether or not they *should* have."

Sami started typing away, her glittery nails clacking against the keys. "Paydirt! One *Cranberry Crush* lipstick, a *Rapturous Rouge* lip liner, and a *Luxurious Lavender* Sachet delivered to Charlene Hamilton on December 7."

"You're my hero, Sami!"

"So now can they get a search warrant, collect all Charlene's lipsticks and find out if one is missing?"

"Sami, we officers call this *CSI Syndrome*. For starters, no judge in his right mind is going to sign off on a search warrant for us to go look for something that *isn't* there. And beyond that, there isn't anything that escalates this case to a level worthy of that kind of investigation."

"Why not? Isn't something missing sometimes just as telling as something you find?" Samantha asked.

"Sometimes, but before you invade and ransack someone's home, you have to have more proof than just that they bought a lipstick and it might be missing."

"We have over 200 colors. If I check my database, I'll bet I find that there aren't more than five *Cranberry Crush* lipsticks that I've sold in this area in the last year. *Crimson Tide* is by far the more popular red."

"They might have been able to dust it for fingerprints and link it to Lloyd or his sister that way, but it was wiped clean."

"Can't you send it to the crime lab and see if there were any epithelials, you know, if any of her skin cells were on the lipstick?"

He laughed. "I'm not the only one in the family watching the cop shows, am I?"

She blushed. "Okay, sometimes when Karl has one on, I'll watch it with him."

"If it was a multiple homicide, maybe we would have been scraping lipstick off the mirror and testing it for skin cells or DNA. Think of it like going to the doctor. When you go in with a sore throat, they're not going to do an MRI because it costs a lot of money to run that test and because it isn't going to tell them what they need to know. They have to do a cost/benefit analysis. Last week we had a lady who wanted us to put out an Amber alert on her Cairn Terrier she thought had been dognapped. Turns out he was over having kibbles at the neighbor's house."

"I was just trying to help." She heaved a giant sigh. "So tell me more."

"It gets better, or I guess I should say it gets worse. They fingerprinted, and besides her fingerprints and the kids and Lloyd's girls, they found Lloyd's fingerprints all over the house. But he had a good explanation for that, because he's been over there sucking up to her doing all kinds of manly handyman repairs in exchange for having her babysit his daughters during their Christmas break from school. And they found my fingerprints from the time I went over and spent time with her so I could try and figure out who was terrorizing her with these phone calls."

"So then you have a reason for your fingerprints being there, too, then, don't you?"

"You'd think. One of the things I did when I was there was go up to her bedroom to look at the cardboard cutout she had standing at the window, because the guy on the phone had said he could see

139

it. I was trying to figure out from the placement of it whether or not he could have seen it from the street or from another neighbor's yard or if he would have had to be in her yard, to know whether this guy was actually watching her house or just toying with her."

"Oh no! Is that the one they found hanging from the fan?"

He stopped and took a couple of deep breaths. "Yes, that's the one. So anyway, my fingerprints were on the cardboard cutout, and they didn't find any of Lloyd's fingerprints anywhere near her bedroom, though I'm sure he wishes that were otherwise. And they didn't find anybody else's on the cardboard cutout besides Lauren and the kids, so whoever did this was smart enough to wear gloves and not leave any fingerprints on the cardboard. I don't have an alibi for the time in question. I've been in her house, so it won't be a stretch to fill the gap and say I found a key and had it duplicated or taped over one of her locks."

"Don't tell me that your fellow officers really believe that you're capable of such a thing!"

"They're just doing their job, Sami. I trust the system. I've seen it work. I trust my fellow officers. I know I'm innocent. I just wish Lauren knew."

"Maybe you need to trust her, too. She's a smart lady. She told me how she negotiated the deal on her house, got a flooring allowance and . . ."

"You don't have to sell me, Sami. She's bright. She's strong. She's confident. But she's also lonely and vulnerable. All of that's magnified during the holidays. There's always a surge in suicides during the holidays, you know."

"I think like you said, ultimately the truth will out. We just have to prove your innocence."

"I don't have to prove my innocence. They have to prove my guilt. It's probably making Lloyd crazy that they haven't arrested me." He continued. "There's more. They apparently found a little clump of fur from a Santa suit. By the way, unless I can get the Santa suit out of the evidence locker by Christmas Eve, you might want to start scouting for a replacement to help your scout friend. I'd get on the phone today to your back-up Santa from church."

"We'll figure something out. I doubt there's a Santa not already booked for Christmas Eve. The girls have elf costumes from a play, so if we need to, they can fill in."

"Good to know." He carried on. "So the day that Lloyd and I both converged to play Santa for Lauren's kids, a cell phone was left behind that has been loaded with calls to Lauren and calls to my cell phone number that makes it look like I've been the one behind the menacing calls. I've been set up and my instincts tell me that troll Lloyd is behind it. Who else could be? And anything I do to warn Lauren or to question his motives and whereabouts now makes it look like I'm a guilty man trying to deflect the blame."

"Oh, Bryan, this is awful!"

"The worst part is that while I'm being questioned, he's probably hanging around being sympathetic and cementing to her the notion that I'm some kind of crooked cop. And then apparently Lauren told the police about a conversation we had. I can't believe she would take it all out of context. After she called me when that phantom guy called and told her he could see her cardboard cutout, she told me how her son had put one of them in the bathtub. Then she went downstairs and was startled by one that her son had moved into the kitchen and thought it was an intruder and picked up something to hit it with."

"Oh, poor Lauren. Her nerves must just be shot."

"I was trying to lighten things up, so I joked about how we needed to get protective detail on the other two. Then she said something about me going to the shooting range, and I said something about being good at offing cardboard culprits and a bunch of other stuff. That's all on record now. And it's probably where he got the idea for this little piece of mischief. I can only believe that she's so shook up about this and messed up and confused that she can't remember the spirit in which I said those things. The only reason she would share that is if she's truly starting to believe I might have done this. That hurts most of all."

"You said don't have an alibi. Where were you?"

"Lloyd's alibi is that he was at the movies."

"Oh, this just gets worse and worse."

"Johnston finally told me he was at the same movie theater coming out of another movie, so he not only has an alibi for the authorities, but she ran into him coming out of the movie, so she thinks there is no way he could be involved. She won't talk to me, and I'm on orders to stay out of it, because I'm a suspect and because of my friendship with the victim, or at least the friendship I once thought I had. I'll bet you dollars to doughnuts Owens set this all up to make it look like I did it, but I don't know how to prove it."

"You still didn't tell me where you were when all this happened."

"I don't have anything anyone can verify. I was Christmas shopping at the mall. You know me. I didn't buy anything, so I don't have a time-stamped receipt from any store to prove I was there."

"That'll teach you to window shop," Samantha said.

"I didn't even buy any gas. I bought a corn dog and a Coke, but I didn't keep the receipt. I didn't see anyone I know who could vouch for me. I was just one of the people lost in the hoard of shoppers. All I can think of is that my fingerprints might be on a bunch of cool stuff at The Gadget Gallery, along with every other gadget geek who has touched that stuff."

"Did you ask anybody a question, like a salesperson, who might remember you?"

"Oh, bless you, Samantha! You're thinking like a cop. I did! I'm trying to remember what it was. I'll bet if I go down to the store it'll jog my memory."

He tore out of the house. Samantha sent a little prayer heavenward for her brother. She watched as his truck sped away toward the mall.

On his way to the mall, Bryan did something he hadn't done since the last tight spot he was in.

"God, it's me, Bryan. I know you think you only hear from me when something's going down, but I'm not asking for me this time. By the way, did I mention how grateful I am that when my gun went off it only grazed my shin? Thanks for that. Really!

Anyway, today I'm asking for Lauren. She won't answer my calls. I'm not supposed to be sticking my nose into this case. Anything I bring up about Lloyd makes *me* look even more guilty. My hands seem to be tied every which way I turn. I'm asking for help, that the information needed will come to light somehow, for me, for her, for anyone else this guy has duped."

He prayed all the way to the mall, pulling in and taking one of the few available parking spots. Bryan sloshed his way through the parking lot and fought his way through the crowds until he finally stood in line at The Gadget Gallery. The line was six deep, but he contained his impatience because he recognized the clerk behind the counter. When it was his turn, he waived the person behind him over to the female clerk. "I need to talk to the other guy. You can go around me."

Bryan was still breathless from his run through the mall. "Do you remember me? You helped me the other day?" That was all he dared say, because the recollection needed to come from the clerk. He could not take a chance of anyone saying he had fed him the information.

"Yeah, yeah, I do remember you. You're the guy who wanted to know about the golf swing analyzer. We talked for quite a bit as I recall."

"Right. You remember me. That's great. There was a crime committed that day for which I'm a suspect, and you're the only one who can place me here at the mall while that crime was being committed."

"Really? I could help solve a crime? I remember, sure. It was Sunday. I had Saturday off, so I remember you. And it was right after I got back from lunch."

"Good. The time is important. Would you be willing to come down to the precinct and make a statement?"

"Sure. And we have security tapes. Some of our high-tech gadgets are easy to shoplift, so we have surveillance in our stores."

"Awesome! I could kiss you." He backtracked. "I *won't*, but I could."

Chapter Twenty-Five

Owens, Lloyd Owens

Lauren only spent one night away from her home, returning home in the morning in time for Lloyd to drop off the girls.

"I might be a little late picking up the girls tonight. Officer Wilmott wants to ask me a few more questions," Lloyd explained. "Don't hold dinner."

You wish. "If you're going to be late, I think I'll just take the kids to McDonald's. We'll start eating healthy again after the new year."

"You, maybe." Lloyd patted his belly. "Don't want to lose my Santa mojo. Ho ho ho."

It illustrated another area of incompatibility that Lauren simply chose to ignore for the present.

* * *

Samantha waited down the street until she saw a white car pull out of the Hamilton driveway with Lloyd at the wheel, the car that Charlene had loaned to Lloyd, giving her an excuse to buy a newer, more luxurious model, a sleek silver Lexus. The Lexus was in the driveway, so Sami figured Charlene was home. She felt a little bit guilty about the little white lie she'd been practicing all morning.

She rang the doorbell, and was almost ready to give it another push when the door opened.

"Samantha! I wasn't expecting you."

"I just thought I'd make a call on my favorite customer."

Charlene invited her in and motioned for her to have a seat at the little table in her breakfast nook. "That's just awful about poor Lauren. I hope they get to the bottom of it all soon."

Let's not go there. "Yes, I hope so, too." She smiled, hoping it didn't look too frozen. "So Charlene, you know I've always taken pride in the high level of quality of the cosmetics of Tara Leigh, which is why I've come to visit you today. It's come to my attention that it's been reported that there may be lead in our lipsticks, in a higher level than is allowable by the FDA. The company hasn't made a statement yet, but this so concerns me that I'm doing a voluntary recall of all lipsticks and giving a full credit for any other merchandise until the studies are completed and I'm positively sure our products once again meet the high standards you've come to expect from TLC."

"*Lead?* Are you sure? What are the ramifications of that?"

"Well, especially for someone like yourself who is always so well-groomed, and never goes out without lipstick on, it could even lead to a minor case of lead poisoning. Someone who swipes a little lipstick on once a week is probably safer. They simply don't have all the answers yet, but I told myself I wasn't going to take any chances with *my* customers. In fact, I'm so concerned, that I'm even willing to take other brands and offer a value comparable to one of our lipsticks, which as you know, cost more than your average department store label."

"Oh my, that's very generous of you! I've got an awful lot of lipsticks, but I don't want them if they've got a dangerous ingredient."

"How long do you think it will take for you to get them all together?" asked Sami.

"Can you give me until tonight? I'll check all the bathrooms and medicine cabinets. I really love your hair care products. Maybe I'll stock up on some of those with my credits."

* * *

Lloyd sat behind the small table. He nodded at the police officer as he came into the little room. "The investigation is proceeding, Mr. Owens. "The piece of fur was indeed a match to the Santa suit owned by Sergeant Everett."

Lloyd nodded. "I'm not surprised."

"And the lipstick used, it was the same brand of lipstick his sister sells. That's pretty damning right there. I guess he could have just grabbed one out of her inventory and she'd never notice it was missing." *And you could have grabbed one of your sister's lipsticks and she wouldn't notice either.*

146

"Exactly! So you're wrapping things up?" Lloyd asked.

"Sometimes the smallest things turn out to be the biggest help." He cleared his throat. "I wanted to ask you about the weather that evening. You said in your previous statement that you followed Mrs. Baylor home from the movie theater. Was it snowing, because we're trying to consider the possibility that the snow might have obscured any footprints left in the backyard. The one thing we're still unclear on is how the house was entered. We didn't find any evidence of locks being taped over, but if the patio door was unlocked, entry would have been from the backyard, and the footprints would have been visible in the snow. However, if the snowfall was sufficient to cover those tracks, we can assume they could possibly have existed. You know, reasonable doubt."

"Oh yes, it was snowing quite thickly, the snow was coming down very strong, very heavy snow, lots of good packing snowman-building footprint-covering snow, which is why I offered to follow Lauren and the boys home, in that snowstorm, severe snowstorm," Lloyd reported.

"We checked the weather report, of course, but that can vary from location to location. I'm sorry to have dragged you all the way down here to discuss the weather. Got to cover all the bases, you know." Officer Wilmott closed his notebook to signify that the interview was over, but his tape recorder was still running.

"So that's it?" Lloyd asked.

"For the most part." He paused, linking his fingers and extending his hands outward to crack his knuckles, a little trick a seasoned cop had taught him. The theory was that the sound of popping knuckles signified a show of force and intimidated a suspect on a subconscious level. "So, you went to see *Skyfall*. How'd you enjoy it? Off the record, who's your favorite Bond girl?"

"Oh, Halle Berry, hands down. Coming out of the ocean in that orange bikini . . ."

"This latest bond Girl is a contender, if you ask me, but of course, I don't go to James Bond movies just for the babes. I do it for the gadgets and the suspense. You can't beat a good suspense scene. My wife says I'm an adrenaline junkie. Maybe it's an occupational hazard. I love it when there's a scene like the one with that explosive device hidden in the cello. You know Bond will come through, but how he comes through is always ingenious, in this case seconds before the entire orchestra would have been blown to smithereens, right?"

"Right!" Lloyd nodded. "Oh yeah, that part definitely had me on the edge of my seat."

"Who comes up with this stuff? Imagine hiding a bomb inside a musical instrument. That was masterful how they built the suspense, going from one instrument to another, while you're bracing yourself for it to either make music or explode. Personally, I thought the bomb was going to be discovered inside the drum."

"Hey, that would have been good, too. One good thump and it's *sayonara.*"

So anyway, I've taken up enough of your time, but one last question. Roger Moore, Sean Connery, Pierce Brosnan or Daniel Craig?"

As Lloyd left the room, Officer Wilmott picked up his notebook and studied it. *Well, Mr. Owens, you're right that it was snowing hard enough to obscure footprints. You fell all over yourself telling me how hard it was snowing, but you have no idea what went on in the middle of the latest James Bond movie.*

Officer Wilmott walked over to his partner's desk after Lloyd Owens had left the building. "Hear me out on this one, Johnston. Owens knows Mrs. Baylor is headed to the movies. He shows up at the same theater, less than two miles from her home, buys a ticket to a movie that gets out about the same time as hers, buys a popcorn, goes into the movie. Then he leaves. She's not aware of that because she's in a different movie with her kids. He would have had plenty of time to drive to her house, string up the cardboard guy, write on the mirror with his sister's lipstick, head back to the movie and get back in with his ticket stub. As the movies end, he then conveniently runs into Lauren and the boys in the lobby. She's convinced he's been there the whole time, and he engineers it so he follows Lauren home so he can be there to comfort her in her hour of need. Not only is he *not* the culprit in her eyes, but he's positioned himself as the hero."

"Hmmm. That *is* plausible. How we gonna make it stick? The phone's got to be key to all this. If we could find out who was behind the harassing phone calls, we might be able to get him to flip on Owens. One thing that doesn't add up is when Mrs. Baylor said the calls started and when this disposable phone was activated. Let's start there."

Chapter Twenty-Six
My Kingdom for an Alibi

Samantha heard the unmistakable sound of Bryan's truck pulling up in front of the house. He burst in the door, this time in better spirits than the last time.

"Any luck?" She motioned for him to join her on the sofa.

"You're now looking at the proud owner of an alibi!" He raised his fisted hands triumphantly.

"Oh, did I miss the sale on those on Black Friday?" She dog-eared the page in the book she was reading.

He strode back and forth in front of the sofa, enthusiastically telling the story. "The guy remembered me, but even better, they had a surveillance tape. It's kind of embarrassing, actually, shows me dorking around with a bunch of products at the store, using the massage chair, all kinds of stuff, but it puts me at the store during the time the crime was committed, for a long enough time and at a mall far enough away that I could not have ducked out and done the crime. The employee from the store is going to make a statement tomorrow morning."

"Then what?"

He finally calmed down enough to join her on the sofa. "That should be enough to clear me. All the rest is circumstantial evidence. I've been checking around about Lloyd and got Ryan Hamilton to admit off the record that he's been paying Lloyd under the table, so maybe we can add a little tax evasion to whatever else they charge him with. And Ryan had a hunch about one of his workers, who was always broke and looking for overtime pay, who suddenly seemed to have an alternate source of income. Wilmott and Johnston are talking to him. If he's the phone guy, they're going to see if they can get him to flip on Lloyd. Ryan apparently isn't as pro-Lloyd as his wife is and they'll probably interview him, too."

"Charlene is going to be devastated. She was so happy to have her baby brother back."

"He fooled a lot of people. So now maybe Lauren will consider that perhaps it's better to be with a guy who doesn't go to church but who tries to be a decent person than a holy hypocrite who never misses a meeting."

"Those aren't the only two choices, you know. There is a subset of the two."

"Do you think she'd want a scoundrel who doesn't go to church?"

"Very funny! Why did you quit going, Bryan? I've never really known."

"I was pretty mad at God after Dad died, after everything that happened that year, with the breakup with Kayla, too. All our prayers for healing, for him to get a heart in time, when it came down to it, none of that made any difference."

"It's funny how that event had a profoundly different effect on each of us. It was after Dad's funeral that I resolved to try and be a better person, try and be a better disciple. And you decided to pack it in on religion altogether."

"I was too young to lose my father. I still needed him."

"Tell that to Lauren's little boys." She reached over and touched his arm. "Remember Jonathan's talk about Dad? I can remember it, almost word for word. I asked him for a copy of it, and I read it sometimes, you know, when I get a little overzealous in my quest to win a TLC trip to Hawaii." She laid her hands, one over the other, on the top of the book. "Remember the part about Dad being in line for a heart transplant?" She stared off into the distance and began to speak from the memory of having read the talk many times over.

"Ben never got to the head of that line. He stands in a different line now a line where those who were first are last and those who were last are first. There are a few people behind him, important people, wondering how come he's in front of them.

'Who's that?' they whisper. 'What's he doing in front of us?'

'I don't know. He's just some high school history teacher from Colorado. He's still got chalk marks on the back of his pants from leaning up against the chalkboard.'

Someone taps him on the shoulder and he steps aside to let the important people pass. At that moment the clouds part, and our Lord calls his name. One of the important fellows can't help but ask. 'Excuse me, but why is he at the head of this line?'

'Because he knew the janitor's name.'"

"I remember. That was a great talk," Bryan said.

"Then he told that story about the teacher giving the test to his students and asking them if they knew the janitor's name. He said that Dad was the kind of teacher who might have given that kind of a test to his students, but instead of giving them the test, he taught them the lesson, because Dad didn't just know the janitor's name. He knew the name of the janitor's children, and which of them played football and which of them wanted to learn to play the violin. He knew where the janitor lived, because he had given him a ride home once when his car broke down. He said that for all we knew, he was the one who slipped an envelope full of money to repair his car into the janitor's lunchbox when he wasn't watching."

"It's a wonder that somehow our family had everything we needed on a school teacher's salary, because Dad couldn't see someone's lack and not share, not do something about it," Bryan said. "Don't you remember more than a few times as a kid getting roped into being the undercover delivery person?"

"Oh, totally!" Samantha began quoting word-for-word again. "'I don't know that. You don't know that, because Ben Everett was the kind of guy who did things quietly when no one was watching. We can't recite a list of his good deeds because he didn't recite them to us. But now that he's gone, don't be surprised if people come forward and share things he did for them, or things that they suspect he was behind.'"

"You have reread that talk a few times." Bryan wiped at his eyes. "I wanted him at the head of the *other* line."

"We *all* did, Bryan. We all wanted him to get a transplant in time. But he didn't. The Lord giveth and the Lord taketh away. Blessed be the name of the Lord." She moved a little closer to her brother. "There's a saying 'Don't cry because it's over. Smile because it happened.' We can rail at God for the thirty or forty or

153

fifty years we'll have to live without our father, or we can be grateful for the thirty or forty years we had with him."

"I guess when you compare me to little Brett and Dirk, I ought to be grateful," Bryan said. "It was just hard for me to keep believing when so many things went wrong."

"Do you ever pray anymore, Bryan?"

"Sure, when something's going down on the job, I shoot a little 'Help!' to the heavens."

"Do you feel like it makes a difference?" Samantha asked.

"Do I think it makes a difference? There have been times I have to say that yes, there had to be providence at work."

"You weren't listening. I said do you *feel* it makes a difference. It's when you start to think about it and analyze it that you get so you can't feel it anymore. Just like you tell me how in police work you have to mesh your instincts with the actual evidence. My instincts tell me that there's something bigger than all of us. And from time to time I get enough evidence that I'm able to keep believing."

"It has been a long time since I've felt anything spiritual. I'm sorry, Sami, but that's just the way it is with me now. God's not returning my calls."

"How many have you made lately?"

"Hey, I prayed on the way to the mall."

"And now you have an alibi."

"Yes, but Lauren's still off somewhere trusting Lloyd and . . ."

"You can't judge God for the times He doesn't answer your prayers or when He doesn't follow your script. You have to believe in Him because of the times He does answer and for the times He gives you something you haven't even asked for. It's those weekly visits to church that give me the strength to keep believing and hang on. When I feel alone and abandoned, there are always things I can call to mind, times when my prayers were answered, things I can't write off as coincidence. I pull those out and use them to hang onto to get through the rough times."

"You out of all of us have always been the strongest. I don't know how Mother would have survived if she hadn't had you to lean on," Bryan said.

She wiped at her eyes. "I just want you to know that in the tug-of-war for your soul, I'll always be pulling on the Lord's side. I won't ever let go of my end of that rope, no matter how much it looks like the other side is about to pull us over the line, because I believe I've got angels pulling on my side, some that we know."

"I guess I have a couple of faith-promoting things I could pull out," Bryan admitted. "But then you have a year where your fianceé dumps you for a guy who makes more money than you do and doesn't have a dangerous job, your dad dies, and just when you're at your lowest point, your gun goes off when you're putting it back in your holster and you shoot yourself in the leg. You start to doubt that God is really there. Or if He's there, you realize He certainly likes everybody else better than He likes you." He paused. "And don't give me that 'whom the Lord loves, He chastens' crap."

Samantha decided it was a good time to change the subject. "Jonathan talked about the Santa suit, too. Do you remember that part?"

"Of course I do. He talked about how Dad paid way too much for this super-deluxe Santa suit to make a little extra during the school break playing Santa, like his father had, but how for every paying gig he got, he had ten more freebies, and how it took about fifteen minutes before it wasn't about money anymore," Bryan said.

"He said that given how much he spent on the suit, he wasn't sure Dad ever even made back his investment," she added. "When Mom gave you the Santa suit, you joked about it being your inheritance. It is, you know."

"And I've made it profitable, for sure. My *inheritance* is currently in the evidence locker at the Boulder Police Department. It hasn't exactly brought me good luck so far, has it?"

"And it didn't bring Dad what he thought it would when he bought it. The fat lady hasn't sung yet, Bryan."

Chapter Twenty-Seven

Out of Our Hands

B ryan looked out the peephole in his door before he opened it, wondering if Officers Wilmott and Johnston were paying him another visit. To this surprise, he saw his smiling Sister Samantha through the peephole.

"Sami, come in! You never visit me here. I always come to your house. What gives?"

She opened an oversized tan leather bag and poured out at least fifty lipsticks onto his coffee table, shoving the remote control off to the side.

"What's this?"

"Charlene's lipsticks. Every single one from her entire house as far as I can tell. The woman's loaded, but I tell you, she can't pass up a bargain. I went online and found out that some lipsticks have been recalled because of lead content so I made up a little white lie and . . ."

"Sami! That's so not like you."

"I know. I've been feeling plenty guilty. I feel sort of responsible for this whole mess in a roundabout sort of way. I'm the one who introduced you to Lauren. The least I could do was a little detective work of my own. I told her I'd take all brands in return for credit, just to make sure she didn't overlook anything."

"So what's the plan now?" Bryan asked.

"Well, I figured we'd go through them all and see if there's a *Cranberry Crush*. And we need to hurry. I've got one more gift I've got to pick up."

"You realize that won't prove or disprove anything definitively, don't you Sami?"

"Not to the police. But it will give *you* another important piece of information. Maybe something you can take to Lauren. Besides, I put my professional reputation on the line for you, so start sorting lipsticks, Sergeant."

Sami could tell that Bryan was tuning her out as she discussed the various shades and brands of lipsticks.

"Smell this one, Bry. Now smell this one. See how much better ours smell?"

"Nobody wants smelly lips," Bryan agreed.

"Don't patronize me, baby brother." She surveyed the table. "This is such a waste of good lipstick. There isn't anything wrong with our lipsticks, you know. Tara Leigh is one of the few cosmetic companies that holds itself to a more rigid standard than required by law when it comes to its ingredients."

"So, no *Cranberry Crush* yet, sis?" He watched as Samantha opened a pink cosmetic bag and poured out five or six lipsticks. "I wonder what brand these are. She said she found these in the guest bathroom and figured they weren't Lloyd's so she might as well cash them in. I suppose I should give her back the cosmetic bag. Then again, it isn't up to her standards. She probably doesn't want it back again, didn't say she wanted it back, but I suppose I ought to at least offer or . . ."

She picked up one of the lipsticks and pulled off the silver sequined top. "Kind of pretty, in a tacky sort of w . . . What? This isn't a lipstick. It's a flash drive. Look, Bryan!"

"They make flash drives in lipstick cases? Jeez! Can't you women just have a normal flash drive, a normal anything?"

She pulled the tops off the other five lipsticks, revealing five more flash drives.

"Bryan, you just put on your cop face."

"Sami, did I hear you say that this bag came from the bathroom that Lloyd is using? Doesn't it strike you odd that a man would have a bag of lipsticks?"

"Oh, she didn't think they were his, obviously or she wouldn't have tossed them into the mix. They were probably left there by someone. . ."

Bryan started talking to himself. "If a woman was keeping her files on lipstick flash drives, wouldn't she keep them near her computer? Why would you keep something that wasn't really a lipstick in the place where you normally would keep a real lipstick?"

Sami pursed her lips. "I don't know. Because you didn't want anybody to know it wasn't really a lipstick."

"Exactly! That old 'hiding in plain sight' thing.

He jumped up from the table and came back momentarily with his laptop computer. He plugged one of the drives into an open port and pulled up a list of files. He clicked on one of the files and a message popped up telling him he didn't have the engineering software necessary to open the file. He scanned the names of the files again but they meant nothing.

"Sami, Karl's an engineer. On your computer at home, hasn't he got all kinds of engineering software?"

"Oh yes! Those programs are so expensive, but he has to keep up with all the latest software. The kids and I, we don't touch his computer, though. We just stay out of his home office, period."

"Well, you're going in there today. I'll take full responsibility for whatever happens."

"You do it, then. I never touch his printer either. It takes up half the room. It looks like one of those quilting machines."

Samantha scrambled to get all the lipsticks back into the bag.

"Forget the lipsticks, Sami, all but these six. Let's get over to your house."

.

A few minutes later, Bryan stared hard at the engineering drawings that came up on Karl's computer screen. His mouth dropped open. "Holy . . ." Sami, the sole proprietor of the swearing jar since she was a teen-ager, her second stream of income after her lucrative cosmetics business, fixed him with a threatening stare. ". . . Samhill."

"Holy Samhill! One of Dad's favorites. Nice save, but that'll be ten bucks for taking my name in vain."

"Sami, swearing is the least of my concerns right now." He grabbed a wad of cash from his pocket and peeled off a ten dollar bill and tossed it her direction. Then he threw in a twenty. "There! Now I'm paid up for the next two times. You used to charge me fifty cents."

"Inflation." Ever the opportunist, she pocketed the money. "So what is that a drawing of? I can never make heads or tails of those technical drawings."

He became solemn. "Something that's got to be very valuable to someone. I think I know who. The less *you* know, the better. Sami, I want you to get in your car right now, get Karl and the kids and go check into a hotel and call me when you get there." He grabbed her and planted a kiss on her forehead."

"But it's Christmas Eve," she protested.

"I don't want to scare you Sami, but someone would kill for what's on these flash drives." A horrible thought occurred to Brian as he said that. *Maybe he already did. Maybe that's why his ex-wife has vanished into thin air. Maybe she found out what he was doing.* "You may have just inadvertently solved a major crime. I'm going to put a protective detail on your home and your family. I hope Charlene isn't aware of what she gave you. She could be in danger, too, but Lloyd might not realize they're missing right away. We can only hope he thinks the bag is still in a drawer in the bathroom or wherever it was. Call me when you decide where to go. I'll have a couple of officers meet you. They'll know what to do from there."

* * *

Lieutenant Glenn Turner looked up as sergeant Bryan Everett burst into his office.

"Everett, I've got good news. You're off the hook as a suspect. Your alibi checked out and none of the other evidence was compelling enough to . . ."

"We've got to call the FBI."

"You know then?"

"Know what?"

"About Lloyd Owens. They ran all the fingerprints they found at Mrs. Baylor's home through the national database. A one *Phillip* Lloyd Owens, Jr. is wanted for custodial interference in regard to his two daughters, Hannah Marie Owens and Elizabeth Kathleen Owens, after taking them from their mother, Marisol Owens of Detroit, Michigan and . . ."

160

"Whoa! He took his daughters from their mother? And not in Florida? I knew he hadn't been in Florida lately. Okay, so the FBI would be involved because he took them across state lines." He took a deep breath. "I've got something else I think they'll be interested in." He opened the cosmetic bag and dumped out the contents onto Lieutenant Turner's desk.

"*Lipsticks?* Look, I know we got that anonymous tip about Mrs. Hamilton and her favorite shade of lipstick from someone who may or may not be related to you and who may or may not sell cosmetics, but we've got bigger fish to fry. Though Mr. Owens managed to disappear from Michigan with his daughters in tow, find work where he was paid under the table and has been driving a car licensed to his sister, he opened himself up to a full investigation when they lifted his fingerprints from the Baylor home. The man is wanted for trade secret theft, for selling plans for hybrid cars to China to the tune of about forty million. He was under suspicion in Michigan, which is apparently when he fled with the girls. The missing link has been finding the files. They're obtaining a search warrant for the Hamilton home as we speak."

"These aren't *lipsticks.*" He picked one up and removed the outer case. They're flash drives full of detailed plans for automotive hybrids. They came from the guest bathroom at Charlene Hamilton's home, a bathroom used by her step-brother, Lloyd, from, did I hear you say, Detroit?"

Lieutenant Turner sprang back as if Lloyd had dumped a nest of pit vipers onto his desk.

"How did you get these? You had no search warrant for their home. You're not even on this case. Where the holy hell did you get these, Everett? And how did you get two steps ahead of the bloomin' FBI?"

"I didn't obtain them illegally. That's all you need to know right now." It only took a moment for Bryan to consider further ramifications of the additional news about Lloyd. His immediate thoughts were of Lauren and the boys. "Lauren's in danger. If he finds out we've got the flash drives, there's no telling what he'll do. I've got to warn her."

161

"His sister and her husband are cooperating. If you say anything to Mrs. Baylor, you could jeopardize your job and jeopardize the entire outcome of the case," the Lieutenant warned him. "And you could put her in the middle of it and compromise her safety. I'm sure the FBI is taking steps to protect her."

"But we don't know that for sure, do we? Those pencil necks won't move until they've all their ducks in a row." Bryan stood up and pounded his fist against a nearby file cabinet. "He's unstable when it comes to her. The guy's not exactly a criminal mastermind. He was smart enough to steal all these plans from his employer, but didn't even bother to put password protection on the files because he thought he'd hidden them so cleverly. Then in his jealousy over a cardboard soldier, he led the authorities right to him. Are they close to an arrest? I can't just sit here and do nothing knowing that low-life has her complete trust. It's Christmas Eve. For all I know, she's with him right now. There's got to be something I can do."

Lieutenant Turner swiveled in his chair to address the Sergeant. "Sure. You can pray."

"I'm not about to just sit around praying, Lieutenant! I'm going undercover! The FBI won't even know I'm an officer. Give me back my Santa suit!"

Everett, I've got to contact the FBI with this new development. I'll release the Santa suit only on the condition that you not interfere with this investigation. Do I make myself clear? Your career depends on it."

* * *

Back in his truck, Bryan decided to take the lieutenant's advice. *It never hurts to have God as backup.* It wasn't the first rushed prayer he'd sent heavenward from his vehicle lately.

"Okay, God. It's me Bryan. Again. I figure you've got some kind of celestial Caller ID so you don't need a last name. I know You're God and You get to pick and choose when to say 'yes' and when to say 'no' and how You go about things, but I'm hoping You won't choose right now to have a Power Trip or teach me some lesson that I probably won't get anyway. You know I've been mad at you for some other stuff, and I've probably broken at least a couple of the more minor Ten Commandments, but I've busted a few people breaking some more serious ones, so maybe it all comes out in the wash. How about if You and I let bygones be bygones? I need Your help protecting Lauren from Lloyd. She trusts him. If there's anything You can do to give her some little inkling into who Lloyd really is, to help keep her and the boys safe from this scoundrel, please . . . I'm counting on You." He swerved to avoid a dog that appeared out of nowhere. "Amen."

And if you want to have Lauren fall into my arms at the end of all this, I'll consider it a Christmas bonus.

Chapter Twenty-Eight

Delivering More than Cookies

L auren headed to the home improvement store, armed with the brand name of the heavy duty deadbolt. It wasn't exactly the kind of last-minute shopping she expected to be doing on Christmas Eve. She was going to buy two more and have Lloyd install them for her, one on the side door leading into the garage and one on the door to the patio. After the intrusion, she wasn't sure she was ever going to feel safe again, but she did know that having a more secure lock on the door between the house and the garage had made her feel safer.

She'd been letting the boys sleep with her in the big king-sized bed so she knew where they were at all times. If anyone wanted her children, he was going to have to go through her. Upgrading all the locks on her doors was a place to start. And Lloyd had ordered a replacement garage door opener that also had an alarm on the remote so that if anyone ducked into the garage while the door was going up or down, you could push a button and sound an ear-piercing alarm.

"May I help you?"

She handed the employee the envelope on which she had written the model of the lock. "I'm looking for another couple of locks like this."

"Those are on aisle ten. Follow me and I'll help you find the one you want."

"Thanks. And do you know which aisle has pet doors? I need one of those, too."

She got sidetracked looking at the Christmas village from *It's A Wonderful Life* and she almost bought the Bailey Savings and Loan when she realized that Lloyd would take that as a sign that she was sentimental about the evening they had watched the movie together. She didn't want to give him any reason to accelerate things. Instead she bought a little Charlie Brown Christmas Tree to set up on the small end table in her living room and hurried home to relieve her babysitter.

* * *

Lauren was pleasantly surprised to answer the door and find Luke Taylor on the porch instead of Lloyd. She greeted her husband's old friend enthusiastically.

"Luke! Great to see you. Come on in."

"Melissa made some cookies for you guys. She's staying close to home now that her due date has come and gone. The only delivery we were hoping would happen today involves a baby. But I know the holidays have got to be hard for you, so I told her I was just going to deliver this one batch of cookies and get back home to spend Christmas Eve with her and the kids."

"Thanks for thinking of us. Tell her I hope everything goes well for her. Remember that if she has a girl, we can do an arranged marriage between her and Brett, so she can be Taylor-Baylor. It's a hard time of year to be pregnant, I'm sure. Both of my boys were born during the summer. I've always thought a December birth would give a woman insight into what it must have been like for Mary, riding a donkey, giving birth in a stable."

"I'll tell Melissa that. She could use a little perspective along about now." He hesitated. "Hey, I wanted to say that as hard as it is for some of us who were especially fond of Kendall, I'm glad to see that you've met someone."

"Come again? I'm sorry. Where did you hear that? It is all around church now, too?"

"Oh, Lloyd helped me with clean-up after the Christmas party. He seems like a great guy, told me all about his little girls. He told me how much he wanted to be a good father for the boys and . . ."

"A good *father* for the boys? We'd only been on *one* date by then."

"Oh, really? He made it sound like you were a lot more serious."

"Things are progressing at a little slower pace than you've been led to believe, but that's all my doing, I assure you. But my feelings for Lloyd are growing, I think. Sometimes it's still a little

166

bit confusing. Maybe you only get one true love in a lifetime, you know. Sometimes I do wonder if I'm trying to talk myself into it, but he's got two little girls who really need a mother, and my boys…"

"I hope it goes well for you. The night of the party he told me how much he wanted to teach them about Kendall, help them honor his memory. We got talking about all kinds of things. I hope he didn't feel bad that I talked about Kendall so much."

She raised one eyebrow. "You talked about Kendall? To Lloyd?"

"Yeah, you know, I told him how crazy he was about you, how he used to say you were his only addiction—you and March Madness."

She spoke slowly. "Do you remember anything else you told him, specifically?"

"Oh, I talked about some old high school stuff. And I told him I was surprised that Kendall had become a medic since he was so accident prone."

"You didn't by any chance tell him about the time Kendall stabbed himself with a screwdriver trying to put together a tricycle, did you?"

"I did. Yeah, I told him that story." He sensed she was growing angry. "Is that a problem?"

"Not for you."

She picked up one of the deadbolts still in the plastic casing, to give her hands something to do. Turning it over, her eyes grew wide.

"Two keys! These locks come with two keys! Locks *always* come with two keys!"

Luke looked at her quizzically. The two-key thing seemed like a big deal to her for some reason. "Two keys are always better than one, aren't they?"

Lloyd has a key to the door between my house and the garage. And I had left the garage door partially up that day for the cats, so he could have gotten in. And my neighbors would not have been suspicious because he's been over here doing handyman stuff so much. The movie thing was all to throw me off. It wasn't Bryan who hung Kendall from the ceiling fan. It was Lloyd!

167

"Not always," she said slowly and deliberately.

"You seem upset. Is everything okay?"

"It's going to be." *EGBOK. Everything's going to be okay.* She stood up and gave him a quick hug. "Love to Melissa. Tell her thanks for the cookies. Someday I'll explain to you what your visit today has meant, but right now . . . I mean, you need to get home to your wife."

"You're sure you're going to be okay?"

"I am. I'm going to be fine."

"You know, Kendall's not the only hero in this family."

That's the same message I felt that night I sat and talked to cardboard Kendall in the living room. There really are communications from the great beyond. It would serve Lloyd right if Kendall really did appear to him, like Jacob Marley appeared to Ebenezer Scrooge.

Tears sprang to her eyes. "Thanks. I do the best I can soldiering on without my soldier."

After Luke left, Lauren dialed Bryan's number. He didn't answer so she left him a voicemail. "Bryan, I'm sorry I haven't returned your calls. I've been wrong about so many things. I hope you can forgive me. I hope you get this soon, because I don't know what Lloyd is going to do next. I just found out that the lock he put on for me came with two keys. He only gave me one of them. Please call me or come over when you get this . . ."

Chapter Twenty-Nine

Santa in the Slammer

Bryan was glad to hear that Sami had been able to cover the Eagle Scout project with her teen-age elves and a couple of undercover helpers. As long as her family was protected, it was good that they were appearing to carry on as would normally be expected.

He drove into the parking lot for the office supply store, dressed in his Santa suit. He had one more present to pick up. He welcomed anything that would keep his mind off just how powerless he felt. He just had to trust that the federal authorities were doing their job. He had to respect those professional boundaries, because he had seen some botched up investigations when people took things into their own hands, not knowing what was really going on or going down.

When he told the cashier what he was there to pick up, she directed him to the photo department in the back of the store. There he found four ladies in various stages of customer assistance. It took a few minutes, but eventually it was his turn.

"How may I help you, Santa?"

"I'm here to pick up a photo gift, a half-size cardboard soldier wearing…"

"Oh, of course, yes. We'll get that right away." One of the ladies retrieved Dirk's new Half-Daddy from the back room. The rest of them gathered around Bryan, emoting as women tend to do. With all the background noise from the Christmas carols playing and the ladies gushing, he didn't hear his cell phone ring.

"This is for the young widow from the news? The one whose house was broken into?"

"I googled her husband and read all the articles about him." Another lady wiped her eyes.

"This is so sweet of you."

He still wasn't sure what kind of a reception he was going to receive at Lauren's house, but he had to try one last time. He could only hope that by the time he arrived, the FBI had made short work of the competition.

He opened the passenger door of his truck and gently set the new Half-Daddy on the seat, draping him with the roll of wrapping paper he'd bought earlier and lapping it over and taping it on the side. He patted the cardboard cutout, content to have it mostly covered. "Sorry, Kendall. Wrapping isn't my strong suit." Before he could get to the driver's seat, his cell phone began ringing. He grabbed it out of the pouch on his belt and flipped it open, giving his standard answer.

"Everett."

"Bryan?" It was Sami. "Charlene just called me, practically hysterical. Some FBI agents were at her house with a search warrant, tearing her house apart and then she said they got a call and just quit abruptly and asked if she knew where they could find Lloyd. She told me she gave them Lauren's address, which was where he was headed. She didn't know what it was about and she called demanding to know because she says she knows you're behind it. She said she cooperated because it was the FBI, but he's still got her convinced that you've framed him somehow."

"That's what I was afraid of. I'm on my way over there, to Lauren's house, but I've been given strict orders not to interfere with the investigation. Whether or not I obey them will depend of what or who I find there. Are you back at the hotel? And the officers are still there with you?"

"Yes, two of them. They're plainclothes. Our room is right by the hotel laundry, and they're in there doing some wash. Can't you please tell me what's going on?"

"Okay, good. Just stay put. You should be safe where you are. This should all be over soon, and then I can tell you everything."

* * *

Lloyd stood on Lauren's porch in his castoff Santa suit. The boys, as usual, clamored to see who was behind the "ho ho ho" and

170

jingling bells. She opened the main door but left the screen door locked and didn't make a move to open the door or invite him in.

He rubbed his hands together. "It's kind of cold out here, Lauren, and as you can see, this suit doesn't offer much protection."

"Oh, it looks like Dirk's shoe is untied. Excuse me a second." She bent down and pretended to tie a shoe that had a Velcro fastener, as she spoke quietly to her oldest son. Reaching over, she pushed the button on a nearby Christmas decoration on the small end table near the door. The animated Santa started dancing and playing *Santa Claus is Coming to Town* on the saxophone. It covered her voice as she spoke to her son. "Go push those numbers Mommy taught you to call on the phone and answer all their questions and I'll get you a new Matchbox car." Because of recent events, she had rehearsed the 9-1-1 calls with Dirk almost every day. He knew their address. He knew his first, middle and last name and he knew his mother's full name.

"Aren't you supposed to come down the chimney, Santa," Lauren said playfully. She needed to keep Lloyd on the porch until the police could get there.

In the background she could hear Dirk answering questions. "My mommy told me to call." She pushed the button again, just as the dancing Santa was winding down. "She's talking to Santa. On our porch." The music drowned out the sound of her son on the phone so that Lloyd couldn't hear, but it also kept her from knowing all of what Dirk was saying. She didn't know exactly how the system worked, but she was pretty sure that whatever he said or didn't remember to say, they would be able to trace the call and would send a squad car.

Lloyd blew on his hands and rubbed them together. "I've got the girls in the car. I thought I'd bring these toys in and then get them out of the car. We're still invited for dinner, aren't we? I've got the heater running in the car but not full blast. It's still cold. I don't want to run down the battery."

She stopped herself from believing his caring dad act, but now she was torn as she thought of the two little girls shivering in the car.

"Here's the thing. Brett's been running a temperature, and I'm not sure I should let you in. I'd hate to pass this around, whatever it is. It could be that nasty flu. I especially wouldn't want the girls to get it. I know this messes up our plans, but . . ."

There was a part of her that wanted to grab that same sharpening steel she had brandished at her cardboard husband and beat Lloyd about the head with it. Her mind raced through all the lies and deceptions, remembering how she had even almost bought his story of a vision from the great beyond.

Vision! I'll give you a vision! There were two keys! You let yourself into my house and you set it up all along to make it look like it was Bryan. You hired somebody to make those calls to terrorize me, and then you were always there to pick up the pieces.

* * *

As the engine of his truck roared to life, Bryan heard a report on his police scanner, a call for response at 933 Gilpin Drive, Lauren's address. He hoped that an officer able to respond was closer than he was, because if he got there first, he knew that he would not put safeguarding his job ahead of protecting Lauren and the boys. He wasn't in an official vehicle, so he couldn't put on his siren and speed through the lights to get there faster. The FBI was supposed to be on the way. But why had there been a call for police response to a 9-1-1-call? It was driving him nuts not to know what was going on. He prayed that someone would get there in time. If Lloyd had taken his own children, what was to stop him from grabbing Lauren's boys and Lauren? *Please, God, whatever is going on, let them be safe.*

* * *

In the distance Lauren heard sirens. She looked over and saw that Dirk was still on the phone. That was good news, if only that it meant they had a lock on the call and could trace where to send the police. She sent the dancing Santa into round three.

She could see by the look on his face that Lloyd's patience was wearing out. "Why do you keep punching that stupid thing?

172

It's annoying. I hate those flapping, screeching, dancing animated stuffed animals."

"Really? I love them. This is an area of our compatibility we haven't really explored. Is this a deal breaker for you? Because I'm kind of a closet dancing hamster fanatic. I thought I had told you that when we were shopping together. We had to take out a loan once to keep me in dancing hamsters. Our attic is one big dance party after dark. There's like 867 of them up there."

Lloyd stamped his feet. "I can tell you're having fun kidding around, Lauren, but why aren't you letting me in?"

"I thought I told you. Brett's sick."

"So you're going to let me freeze to death out here instead?"

"I thought you would have the sense to get back in your warm car, Lloyd. You're the one doing this to yourself, standing out there in the cold. I thought you just wanted to flirt with me a little through the door before you left. My son is sick, like really sick. Contagious sick. I don't know what you think is going to change about that in the next ten . . ."

Suddenly she saw several vehicles turn onto the street, lights flashing. Thinking quickly, she acted surprised. "I wonder what's going on! Get the girls, Lloyd, so they're not scared!" As Lloyd turned to head towards his car, four vehicles came to an abrupt stop and it became obvious to him that Lauren's house was their destination. Thanks to her quick thinking, he was a sitting duck there on the lawn between her front porch and her driveway. Law enforcement officials seemed to pour from the vehicles.

"FBI. Are you Phillip Lloyd Owens?"

Lloyd quietly nodded his head. "Yes, I am."

"Hands in the air where we can see them."

Dirk was looking out the window and Brett was right beside him, watching wide-eyed as a subdued Santa quietly surrendered to the men in black. In the rush of excitement, Lauren had forgotten about shielding her sons from the current spectacle and it was too late now. She wasn't sure damage control was even possible anymore.

Lauren looked over at Dirk. *What did he say to get the FBI to come? Maybe I should get him two Matchbox cars.*

173

A man in a black uniform handcuffed Lloyd. Her blood ran cold at words she heard. "Phillip Lloyd Owens, Jr., you are charged with custodial interference for removing Hannah Marie Owens and Elizabeth Kathleen Owens from the care of their mother, Marisol Rodriquez Owens of Detroit, Michigan, for conspiracy to make telephonic threats to Lauren Baylor of Boulder, Colorado, and there is a small matter of international trade secret theft from your former employer, General Motors." She saw Lloyd's head jerk up at that. Whatever else they had on him, he hadn't been prepared for that one. She stepped out onto the porch, intending to go to the car and try to shield the girls from further trauma.

She almost didn't recognize the harsh voice that came from the man in handcuffs as he turned in her direction, unrestrained anger flowing from him. "We could have had it all, Lauren. Do you have any idea what you missed out on? Tens of millions of dollars. It could have all been ours, yours and mine if you had just played your cards right. We could have been so happy. We could have gotten away from this freezing cold and moved to the tropics. We could have had a new life anywhere we chose. I could have given you *everything,* Lauren. I was so close. I could have given your boys everything they ever wanted or needed."

By then it was too dark for her to look him in the eyes, nor did she want to ever again, but her voice cut through the darkness and went straight to his heart. "No, Lloyd, you could never have given them the one thing they need the most, the thing they lost, and the thing that I want and need for them. The thing that they need most is a kind, decent, hardworking, unselfish man to look up to." She turned away from him. "Goodbye Lloyd, or whoever you are."

Lauren watched as Lloyd, in his threadbare Santa suit, was taken into custody and loaded into the back of a black van. Her thoughts turned again to the car in the driveway and the two shell-shocked little girls watching their father be led away in handcuffs. She could hear their muffled cries coming from the backseat of the car. A female agent standing near the car spoke to Lauren.

"I'm Agent Michelle Wheaton. I'm sorry they had to see that, but we couldn't risk tipping him off by trying to get the girls out of the car first. The agents did the best they could to keep it from becoming a neighborhood spectacle, but arresting Santa on Christmas Eve does tend to draw attention." At that, Lauren looked up and saw curious neighbors on their porches or looking out their windows. But she couldn't worry about what the neighbors thought. Not when there were four little kids to worry about.

"What's going to happen to the girls? It's Christmas Eve. They can stay here with me and my sons, at least until Charlene or someone can get here. I've even got a few gifts for them. I don't know what your procedure is. I just don't want them to spend Christmas Eve down at the police station or FBI headquarters or in some temporary foster home where they don't know anyone."

"I think they're going to be all right here in just a few minutes." Agent Wheaton opened the back door of the car and the two little girls climbed out and hugged Lauren around the legs.

"You're going to be okay, Katie, Marie." She patted them both on the back as they hid their faces and sobbed. "People who love you are going to take care of you and make sure everything is going to be okay."

Lauren was so busy talking to Agent Wheaton and comforting the girls that she didn't notice one of the agents walk around his car and open the back door, as if he were on a date. A woman with long dark hair emerged and ran across the snow calling the names of her daughters.

"Hannah! Lizzie!"

As soon as she heard her name, Hannah Marie turned and flew into her mother's open arms, followed by her sister. The force of both of them both knocked their mother over into the snow, and the three of them cried and kissed and hugged.

"It's you! It's really you!"

"Mommy! You *didn't* forget about us!" The three of them were locked in a group hug so tight that you could not tell where one left off and the other started.

"Merry Christmas, Mrs. Owens." Agent Wheaton turned to Lauren. "We've been looking for Owens since he left Detroit on the trade secret theft charges. Not to take anything away from

175

solving a major case, but this . . ." She gestured toward the mother and her daughters. "This was what I was waiting for."

Lauren could tell that reuniting the mother and her daughters had been one FBI agent's Christmas miracle. She wondered where the three of them were going to spend the night."

"If they need a place to stay, please let them know my home is available."

"We've made arrangements at a hotel, but that is kind of you, Mrs. Baylor."

"Will you please give—what was her name?"

"Marisol."

"Marisol. Will you give her my number in case she needs anything. I'm sure it's on file somewhere. I don't have a paper on me. Lloyd said her name was Amber."

"As in *Amber Alert*? The guy must have thought he was pretty clever with that one," Agent Wheaton said. "Here's my card. You can email your number to me, and I'll pass it along."

Lauren almost offered her hospitality again, sure that a home was better than a hotel on Christmas Eve, but she realized that it might be better to give them their privacy. It wouldn't really matter where they were, because wherever it was, they had the gift of being reunited.

Chapter Thirty

Third Time's the Charm

L auren was so caught up in watching the tender scene before her that she didn't even notice when a black truck pulled up and parked in front of her next-door neighbor's house. Bryan could see that there were more than enough law enforcement officers and FBI agents on the scene and that he wasn't really needed, at least, he observed, not in any kind of official capacity.

He waited in his truck, running the heater and the radio, listening to Christmas carols and waiting for the police business to be wrapped up. He pulled out his cell phone and noticed he had a new message. Listening to the message from Lauren, he felt fresh hope fill his soul.

As the last police car drove away, Bryan climbed out into the chill night air. With a green burlap bag in one hand, and a cardboard replacement dad in the other, he headed up the walk to Lauren's house. He leaned the cardboard cutout against the wall out of sight.

It was the third time that month Bryan had stood on Lauren's doorstep dressed in the red suit. His "ho ho ho" brought two little boys scampering to the door, followed by their mother.

Lauren, as always, was quick to do she could to salvage the situation for her little boys. "Are you a *good* Santa, because there was just a Santa here earlier who wasn't a good Santa and…"

Dirk picked up the story. "The storm troopers put him in a car and took him back to the North Pole. Did you know that even Santas can be naughty or nice?"

Bryan smiled. He knelt down to be on Dirk's level as he had seen Lauren do so many times. "I do know that. I've got a secret, Dirk. *Bad* Santas go to the South Pole. They don't have reindeer there, so they can't get out and fly away and hurt people ever again." He stood up and whispered to Lauren. "*And penguins peck their eyes out.*"

At the sound of a familiar key word, little Brett pulled out one-fourth of his vocabulary. "Woodolph."

Bryan stood back up and spoke quietly to Lauren. "From what I understand, the bad Santa could have a white beard for real growing by the time they let him out."

"Yeah, it sounded like his Christmas goose is cooked. You'll have to tell me all about what he was up to sometime, and how this all came about, but I'd really rather not think about *him* right now."

"I like the sound of that," Bryan said.

Her tone turned flirtatious. "So tell me again why I should let you in, Santa?"

"Because they say the third time's a charm. And because I come bearing gifts. And just in case I need it, I have a note from my sister, who is your friend, and who wants you to know she will vouch for my good character and also that she's not completely responsible for everything contained in my pack herein, that your church friends all love you but please don't let them know you know this stuff was from them, because they're trying to get brownie points so they can all go to heaven." He stopped to take a breath. "She also wants to remain anonymous as the instigator of this visit, although if you find any gifts of a cosmetic nature for which you would like eventual replacements, I'm sure she'd be glad to hook you up."

Lauren laughed, and Bryan could not help but notice that momentarily her eyes did not look sad. Again he'd managed to banish the blues from her green eyes. That alone had been worth the trip. She opened the door and he went inside, setting down his pack and the gift that was too big for the burlap bag.

Santa began to take gifts out of the bag, examining the tags and dividing them up between the two little boys. Brett wordlessly took his gifts, as always, taking in everything that was going on. Dirk was wound to a fever pitch. Santa contemplated Lauren's youngest son.

"The little guy doesn't say much yet, but I've noticed that he watches everything, doesn't he? I wouldn't be surprised if he just starts talking in complete sentences one of these days."

"Oh, thank you for saying that, Santa! My mother is worried because he isn't talking yet, but he understands everything I say to him. Lots of people want to tie it to what happened, but my counselor says to ignore them, that he's probably developing on the right time schedule for him, especially if this isn't a big deviation from his personality before . . . you know. My mother-in-law says he just has an old soul and I agree with her. He's always been kind of a serious little guy. Even as a baby he was serious, didn't laugh or babble a lot. I used to just look into his eyes and ask him who was in there."

"I'm sure that when you finally find out, it'll be a wonderful revelation."

"You know what? I think I'm going to let the boys open these gifts tonight. I think it would be nice if you could report back to Samantha that the boys enjoyed their gifts."

"I'm in. I haven't got anywhere else to go." Lauren gave him a stern look. "I mean we'd better hurry and open these presents so I can fly around the world with my reindeer."

"Woodolph," said Brett.

"We've got to have more of these in-depth conversations, buddy. So Brett is a man of few words. There's nothing wrong with that," Bryan said.

The boys tore open their gifts—books and trucks and tub toys, while Lauren and Bryan watched from their vantage point on the nearby sofa. When the feeding frenzy was over, Bryan brought out the big gift he had retrieved from the porch and had slipped behind the sofa, waiting for a time when he had Dirk's attention.

"Dirk, Santa has one more gift for you."

"Santa remembered my name, Mom!"

"See, I told you he wouldn't forget you."

"Don't you have to go all over the world tonight, Santa?" Dirk asked.

"Yes, I do, but I came here first because bringing this to you was my most important job tonight."

Lauren knew immediately what it was when Bryan pulled the odd-shaped, poorly-wrapped gift out from behind the sofa. He set the gift down and Dirk tore into the wrapping.

Bryan had known that this gift was going to make Lauren cry, but he could not contain his own emotions at the little boy's reaction. "He fixed my Daddy! Santa fixed my Daddy!"

Dirk threw his arms around Santa's neck and Bryan knew that forever after if anyone asked about his favorite Christmas memory, no matter how long he lived, this would be it. He hoped in some small way this gift made up for some of the holiday trauma he'd had a part in.

Lauren dabbed at her eyes with the sleeve of her sweater. "How . . .?"

"I just did a little detective work, mostly online, finding out which kind of stores make these and then called around. I figured that chances were good whoever made them still had the files from when Kendall ordered them. When I explained about Dirk, they did it free of charge and put a rush on it. There were all these crying ladies when I picked it up. If you ever want to go by and thank them, I'll give you all the info. You might need to keep it handy in case he gets waterlogged again. I thought they were going to cry all over it and give us a repeat performance."

"I'll definitely go by the store and thank them."

"There's more, but I don't quite know how to explain this to you without sounding like, I don't know, Lloyd," Bryan said.

Lauren shook her head. "You haven't even heard about the vision yet."

"Tell me you're not serious, Lauren. He didn't!"

She nodded her head. "According to Lloyd, Kendall appeared and asked him to look after me. I'll tell you more later, after the boys are out of earshot."

"Sounds interesting. It'll probably make me want to tear him limb from limb. I may not be the most religious guy out there, but I don't use feigned faithfulness and fake visions to accomplish my own selfish purposes."

"So what is it you were about to tell me?" she asked. "The boys look pretty busy with those blocks."

"Speaking of religion, my sister gave me a big pep talk recently about going back to church. I went home and . . ." He stopped. "I know you'd probably never do something quite like

180

this, but I got my scriptures, and I said, 'Okay God, talk to me.' It was more of a challenge than a prayer. I opened to a random page in the Bible and stuck my finger in it, deciding that whatever scripture my finger pointed to would be God's message to me."

"You're right that I've never issued a challenge to God quite like that, but I have had answers to problems come to me that way, just opened to a scripture that fit somehow."

"I told myself that if it was one of those 'Amram begat Jonah' scriptures, I would know God wasn't really mindful of me, I guess. I've experienced a few tough things that I haven't shared with you. They pale in comparison to what you've been through. I had a broken engagement the same year my father died, and then I had an injury in the line of duty. I was angry and bitter for a long time afterwards. I guess I was looking for some proof from God that He still knows who I am."

"So what did the scripture say?"

"Just a second." He pulled his wallet out of his pocket. "I wrote it down." He pulled a out a folded notecard. "It's Proverbs chapter twenty-three, verse ten." He didn't unfold the card. "A little background first. You remember how when I came over to wait for that guy to call so we could try and trace where the call was coming from that you asked me if I would . . . You gave me the cardboard dad that had taken a bath."

"Of course I remember that. That wasn't an easy thing to do. It seemed sad to keep it and equally as sad to throw it away, so I figured that maybe if I could find someone else to do it for me it might be easier. Thanks for handling that for me. And there was always the chance I might scare myself again with it, some dark night in the garage. But what does that have to do with a scripture in Proverbs?" Lauren asked.

He opened the notecard. "This is what my random scripture said: 'Remove not the old landmark and enter not into the fields of the fatherless.'" He leaned over and pulled the leg of his Santa suit out of his boot. "I'm not one of those guys who understands everything backwards and forwards in the scriptures, but this said to me that if there was a way I could replace that cardboard dad for Dirk, I should. And it also told me that God *does* know who I am.

181

I'm not sure what the 'fields of the fatherless' means, but it just seemed to me like a message to accept your past and tread lightly."

She spoke softly. "How could I not see that you were the polar opposite of Lloyd?"

"North Pole. South Pole. You're right! It must have been our matching Santa suits," he said. "I hate it when I show up to a party and another guy is wearing the same outfit." He turned his attention back to Lauren's oldest son.

"Now remember, Dirk, he can't swim."

"Yes, he can! My dad took me swimming all the time."

Bryan turned to Lauren. "Someday maybe I'll get a chance to tell these guys about a special gift I got from my dad after he died, a gift that keeps on giving. I'm afraid I wasn't nearly as grateful as I should have been." He pursed his lips and blinked to fight back the unmanly tears that threatened. "I'll get you the replacement info in case this one takes a bath again. Have you been able to do First Aid on the guy from the bedroom?"

"Actually, I have. They make duct tape in camouflage now, you know. He's braced with a few heavy-duty popsicle sticks, and I've forgiven him for having another women's lipstick on his collar."

Bryan laughed and then turned serious. "Lauren, I have to tell you another thing I admire about you, your resilience." He looked at Brett playing with one of his new Christmas gifts, a collection of little bottom-heavy plastic figures that righted themselves after he knocked them down. "You're like a Weeble."

She smiled. "You mean these pants make my butt look big?"

"Is there a woman alive who hasn't asked that question of a terrified man?" Bryan asked. "I meant that you bounce back, but if you'll turn around, I could give you an answer on the other . . ."

"Santa, behave yourself!"

Time to change the subject. Bryan turned his attention to serious little Brett, who was now intently running a dump truck back and forth on the floor.

"Looks like the truck is a hit. Maybe even a hit-and-run with that purple Weeble."

"If my mother was here, she'd be pointing out that he isn't making the 'vroom-vroom' noise," Lauren said.

Bryan chuckled. "I'm sure there's a kid down the street his same age who's been *vrooming* for months." Bryan reached one more time into his burlap bag. "I've got something special for Brett, too." He handed a red gift bag to the little boy. Brett looked up at Santa as if for permission and then solemnly and slowly lifted a red-nosed reindeer out of the bag.

"Woodolph," he said seriously.

"He has kind of a Darth Vader voice when he says that, doesn't he?" Bryan showed him which button to push to turn the nose on and off.

"Woodolph," Brett repeated again, pushing the button.

"He understood all that perfectly. There's nothing wrong with this kid."

Brett put his new Rudolph in the back of the dump truck and continued driving across the floor. Santa smiled at Lauren and decided now was as good a time as any to ask what had been on his mind. The kids were happily playing once again and not paying any attention to the grown-ups, at least momentarily.

"I know you're still reeling from the fallout from your most recent attempt at a relationship, but I was wondering if you'd have dinner with me on New Year's Eve."

"I won't lie to you, Bryan. I like you, a lot, but . . . I'm just not sure I can allow myself to get involved with someone in such a dangerous profession."

"You wouldn't be the first." He hesitated. "It's just dinner, Lauren."

"When Kendall died, I told myself I could never go through that kind of worry again, not knowing if . . ." She began to cry. "I'm not as much of a Weeble as you think I am. It's all an act. I can fake it for a while now and then. That's all. Emotionally I sometimes feel like I stepped on a land mine, too, and have been ripped apart. If we got serious, I would have to live every day wondering if you were going to die."

"And I worry that you're never going to allow yourself to fully live again. I *am* going to die. We *all* are. I could slip in the shower on my manly Tara Leigh bar of exfoliating soap. It's dinner, Lauren, only dinner. If New Year's Eve isn't good, we could go for, um, three months from this Friday, as long as I can get on the calendar. I can be patient. Yes, what I do can be dangerous, but it can also be boring and uneventful." He lifted his pant leg and showed her a scar about three inches long, just above his black Santa boot. "I've already been shot, you see, so statistically I'm good, got that out of the way. You can't let fear be your default mode."

"Oh, my goodness! What happened?"

"The bullet just grazed me. It isn't even worth describing. Well, I could, but trust me, in the hero line-up in this house, I'd look pretty ridiculous."

"You told me never to trust anyone who says 'trust me.'"

"Okay, I shot myself in the leg. As usual I'm my own worst enemy."

"*What?*"

"I was putting my gun in the holster and it went off. It was a hair trigger." He smiled and continued. "There's another possibility I've been looking into, working undercover to help catch predators. I'd be sitting behind a computer, as a decoy, pretending to be a teen-ager. It isn't physically as dangerous but I understand it can kind of mess with your mind. I just wanted you to know that I'll always be willing to consider other possibilities that could take me further out of the line of fire. As Sergeant I'm already in less danger than when I was just an officer. If I was ever promoted to Lieutenant, for example, that would give me even more administrative duties. That is less danger and more money, and a more secure retirement, all of which are good things."

"I appreciate that, but it isn't just that you have a dangerous job."

"There's more?"

"After this whole thing with Lloyd, I told myself I'd take my time with any future relationship. It isn't going to be easy to trust again. I have two little boys I'll have to explain things to further about what happened to their father as they grow older, not to mention whatever their disturbing memories are of this whole

184

crazy Christmas season. I just feel still like it's too soon. I know you said you can be patient, but . . ."

"And the turtle climbs back into her shell?"

She paused, choosing her words carefully. "I told Lloyd I wasn't ready, that I just wanted to be friends. He talked a good game about us being two single parents who could be supportive of each other, but all the while, I felt he was just waiting in the wings for that status to change."

"So you worry that if you say you aren't ready, that I'm going to be trying to up the speed limit?"

"Your sister is right. You do talk like a cop."

"A relationship can only go as fast as the slowest person. One of my favorite things to do as a rookie policeman was to get on the freeway and go the speed limit, with a long line of cars behind me that didn't dare pass me or go any faster than I was. You set the speed limit, and I promise to abide by it. If I have an unexpected burst of speed, just turn on your flashing lights and I'll get the message. All I ask is that you give me a warning for my first offense."

"You're still willing to have a relationship with me, knowing there might be a meltdown coming in August?"

"It might be good to have someone to lean on as that anniversary approaches."

She hesitated and he saw her head go down. He gently reached over and lifted her chin so he could look into her eyes. "I'm not Lloyd. There's a big difference between dumping too much fertilizer on a plant, hovering over it to measure the growth, overwatering it, and prying open the flowers to get them to bloom or taking a plant, giving it a little sun, a little rain, and anything else it needs to grow and standing back to enjoy the flowers. If this relationship is going to grow, it will happen naturally."

"I've been through so much lately. I still feel very fragile, emotionally. I can't believe I was so trusting of someone who . . ."

"Lloyd fooled a lot of people," Bryan said.

"He didn't fool you."

He laughed. "I'd like to claim it has to do with my wonderful insights into people and my trustworthy instincts, but I basically started out just being a jealous guy, hoping there was something I could find that would make him look bad. Something happened to me that day when I stood on your porch and looked into your eyes for the first time. I know that sounds sappy, but it's true. Lloyd thought he could steal the key to your heart the way he stole the extra key to your deadbolt. By the way, I can't believe Wilmott and Johnston didn't pick up on that *key* piece of evidence, pun intended."

"When Kendall died, I couldn't believe I might actually ever be able to love again. Sometimes I'm still not sure, but I was just thinking . . ." She lowered her head like she did when she was about to share something personal. "Maybe . . . maybe my heart is like that deadbolt."

"Double bolted and impenetrable?"

She smiled and raised her head, this time meeting his eyes, willing for a moment to be vulnerable and open to possibilities. "No, maybe it comes with two keys."

"A much better option than mine."

She averted her eyes again. "So what happened to you, on my porch?"

"In a word, I was smitten. I knew I wanted to be the one to make your eyes look happy again. And then I looked back and I saw you kissing Lloyd and my hopes were dashed on the rocks. But I didn't give up hope, because I saw this look on your face that told me you hadn't wanted him to kiss you. I reminded myself that day that the evidence doesn't lie."

"If you had been a fly on the wall, you'd have seen that after you left, I let him have it for that kiss. He totally took advantage because I had said he was my boyfriend, for protection from you, from this strange Santa. I totally didn't want him to kiss me! I could never have imagined kissing anyone besides Kendall, and it was every bit as awful as I had thought it would probably be."

"The man obviously didn't know what he was doing. It looks to me like he just grabbed you and got right to it. The way I see it, kissing a woman is like landing a plane. You don't just drop out of the sky. You make an approach, and you wait for an all-clear from the tower."

As he described the process, Lauren couldn't help but be transported back to Colorado State and the warm fall day when she had first kissed Kendall. Then she found herself trying to remember the last time he had kissed her. She closed her eyes momentarily and was almost startled to open them and see Bryan sitting next to her.

"Sounds like you know a lot about, about . . . flying planes. Do you fly?" she asked.

"Only as a passenger. All I'm saying is that if kissing Lloyd was less than wonderful, perhaps your study could benefit from a larger sample group." This time Bryan was the one averting his eyes. "Is that really true, that you've never imagined kissing anyone besides Kendall? I mean since he died." He suddenly realized he wasn't sure he wanted to hear the answer and quickly switched gears. "Lloyd was a short fat little troll."

"Every time you describe him he gets uglier."

"You're right. He was a short fat little troll with protruding nose hairs. Okay, so I'm not looking at him with eyes of love. I suppose he wasn't a bad looking guy, but people can become better looking or worse depending on their personalities and their actions. Let's face it, though, he filled out the Santa suit way better than I do, without half-a-quilt's worth of stuffing. What do they call it? Batting. So yeah, I'm just saying that I can't imagine any woman, grieving or not, wanting to waste her lip gloss on those pudgy lying lips."

"Please, Bryan, don't make me relive that kiss!"

Lauren decided to change the subject. This talk of kissing was making her self-conscious. And it had started her wondering what it might feel like to kiss Bryan, but she couldn't tell him that, and she certainly couldn't answer his question and admit that she had wondered before what it might feel like to kiss him. She was going to do the responsible thing and rein in those feelings. She couldn't trust them. Maybe she was just latching onto another guy who made her feel safe. Of course she would feel that way about a police sergeant. It was Christmas Eve. She couldn't allow herself to be influenced by the lights on the tree and the Christmas music playing on the radio in the background like she had the second time she'd let Lloyd kiss her. She and the boys were having Christmas dinner at Kendall's parents' home the next day. How would they feel knowing she had betrayed the memory of their son that way?

She looked around for a distraction. "Let's see what's in my stocking." She reached in and pulled out a Tara Leigh lip gloss. She read the label, blushing a little. "Raspberry Rapture." She quickly reached her hand into the stocking again, hoping for something more mundane—some sticky notes, maybe, or a hair scrunchy. It was another lip gloss. "Sensuous Cinnamon." She opened the lid and squeezed a little onto her finger. "Mmmmm. Tastes like a Snickerdoodle," she said, trying to cut back on the uncomfortable feelings permeating the room. At the mention of their favorite cookies, her two little boys came running.

"More Snickerdoodle cookies?" Dirk was immediately at her side.

"Hungwy," said Brett.

Lauren interpreted. "That's his all-inclusive word for food of any sort."

"Efficient system you've got there, young man." Bryan tousled the sandy head.

Beneath his beard, the smile of a Santa who had a sister who loves him grew wider. He gave Lauren a disclaimer, lowering his voice. "This is Lloyd's legacy. I'm suddenly hyper-sensitive to anything that even vaguely looks like manipulation. You do know I'm not the one who . . ."

She inclined her head in the direction of her children. He was Santa. Of course he was the one who filled the stockings. "I mean, I hope you like what I put in your stocking, Lauren." He grinned, testing the water. "You know, I've always loved Snickerdoodles, too."

"Really? We'll have to see what we can do about that." He caught her brief flirtatious smile before she put her poker face back in place. "Now that you mention it, there's a plate of them sitting over there on the table for you. It has been tough keeping the boys out of them, now that they've polished off the rest of the batch."

After the fiasco with Lloyd, she was doing the best she could to be sensible and not allow her emotions to get the better of her.

Just as she reached into her stocking and pulled out another gift, a creamy lipstick with yet another come-hither name, she heard the strains of a familiar Christmas carol. The words floated across the room and hung there, adding to the palpable sexual tension.

"I saw Mommy kissing Santa Claus."

Lauren threw down the lipstick and stormed over to the time-out corner, facing the wall so Bryan would not see her tears. He hesitated for a moment and then went over to her. Gently he took her by the shoulders and turned her to face him. He looked into the green eyes that had turned sad once again.

"It's okay, Lauren. Cry until it feels better."

"What *is* this? *The bloomin' Hallmark Channel?*" She put her head on his shoulder and began to sob.

Dirk picked up the lipstick and brought it to his mother. "Mommy, it's okay. You dropped your present, but I found it," sure that her tears were related to the lost lipstick somehow. Bryan reached out and took it, silently reading the label that said "Peppermint Passion."

Suddenly the humor of it hit him. He tried his manly best not to laugh, but sometimes it's just not possible. Lauren gave him a dirty look and wiped at her eyes, as always wondering how her grief and display of emotions were affecting her little boys. Something quietly whispered to her soul that besides needing a dad they could look up to, they deserved a mommy who smiled sometimes, maybe even one who could still laugh.

"What are you laughing about?" she demanded.

Wordlessly Bryan handed her the lipstick and she read the name.

"This *is* all very Lloyd-like, now that you mention it," she said. "Christmas Eve, the lip gloss, the song . . ."

"I'd certainly agree with you, Lauren, if I . . ." Bryan paused for effect as he looked heavenward ". . . if *I* had been the one who orchestrated it."

Lauren found herself laughing through her tears. "Oh, that's even worse than Lloyd's *humble carpenter* routine."

Dirk looked up at her, smiling. "Aren't ya gonna do it, Mom?"

"Do what?"

"What the song says. Aren't ya gonna kiss Santa Claus?"

It was the final domino for Lauren. Or perhaps it was the next-to-the-last domino. The last domino was when she looked at the Christmas tree and saw a cardboard Kendall propped up next to it with tinsel that had been draped all over him by his young son. A man that would do something like Bryan had done for her little boy, well maybe he *did* deserve to be kissed.

I can do this. She picked up the two lip glosses and one lipstick. "So what'll it be, Santa? Raspberry Rapture, Sensuous Cinnamon or Peppermint Passion?"

Bryan looked at her, speechless.

"What?" she asked. "I'm on approach. Reading signals from the tower. Do I have to make another pass?"

"If this really was *The Hallmark Channel*, wouldn't there be some mistletoe, too?"

"Don't push it, Saint Nick. The runway isn't long enough."

"Okay, Cinnamon. I'd like to compare and see if it's as good as those cookies look. Lay a little sugah on me, honey. I mean, cleared for landing."

It wasn't a long kiss. It was a quick mistletoe kiss, gentle and tentative, as perhaps a first kiss ought to be. Bryan was not without an understanding of what it had probably cost her emotionally to risk and trust even to that extent after the recent events of her life. She met his eyes and he read most of what else he needed to know there, but he asked anyway.

"So?"

"So?" She lifted both eyebrows.

"So, you've doubled the size of your sample group, and I have to admit that I'm curious as to your findings. And don't tell me something nebulous, like better than Lloyd but not as good as

Kendall, because there's a lot of room between those two polar opposites."

"It didn't feel . . . *wrong.*"

"So if it didn't feel wrong, can I assume that it felt . . . *right?*"

"I can see how you might jump to that conclusion. How about you?" she asked.

"I was thinking about how good it felt to be growing closer to you." He paused. "And how it's about time someone gave Santa what *he* wanted for Christmas. And I was wondering if it might have been better with the Raspberry Rapture."

"Don't push it, buddy."

"What were *you* thinking?" he asked.

"You really want to know?"

"No, lie to me." He reached for her hand. "Now I'm not sure, but go ahead."

"First, I was thinking about the possibility that when I have dinner tomorrow with Kendall's parents how mortified I'm going to be if Dirk rats me off and tells everybody that I was kissing Santa Claus and . . ."

"At least you know you can count on Brett to keep your tawdry little secret."

She laughed and put her arms around his neck and looked into his eyes.

"And . . .?" he asked.

"And I was thinking maybe sometime we should try it again, without the beard."

Chapter Thirty-One

Guess Who's Coming to Dinner

Lauren looked down, still afraid she was a little bit flushed from the kiss. "So, I know this is kind of a last-minute invitation, but I was wondering what you're doing tomorrow.

"I was planning on spending the day with my sister's family. Of course Samantha will be going to church. You know, when I was a kid I absolutely hated when Christmas came on a Sunday, because the folks would make us go to church instead of letting us stay home and play with our toys. I mean you wait and wait for Christmas and when it finally gets there, you have to go to *church?* That's pure torture for a kid."

"I remember feeling the same way, as a kid. I think it's going to be a short service, only about an hour, but now I love when Christmas is on Sunday because it gives the day the spiritual center it sometimes lacks."

"Okay, way to make me feel guilty for wanting to stay home and play with my toys. You do that almost as well as my mother."

"Just what a woman wants to hear at the beginning of a relationship, that she reminds a guy of his mother. If you think you could endure a church service, I was wondering if you'd like to come with us." Lauren said.

"Really?" He smiled broadly. "You know, I don't get as many toys as I used to, so I could probably pry myself away. I very much would love to join you. What time should I be here?"

"Around eight. We should probably leave by eight-thirty."

"Do you want to go in my truck? In the extended cab, I can fit the little boys and their car seats, but my observation has been that it isn't the easiest vehicle to get into when you're wearing a dress."

"Have they had you working in drag?"

"I've had a few women in my truck." He backtracked thinking about how that sounded. "I mean, I've had a few woman *ride* in my truck."

She smiled as he fell all over himself trying to recover from his poor choice of words. "Why don't we take my car? That way we don't have to move everything around."

"Won't I be crowding out the guy who usually rides in the passenger seat?" Bryan asked.

"He can ride in the back with the boys in a pinch. We just have to turn him sideways, although he could get picked up for not wearing his seatbelt."

* * *

Lauren felt all eyes were on her as she entered the church building. She had no way of knowing who knew about Lloyd. She hoped, if only for Charlene's sake, that word had not spread like wildfire, but with the news coverage and church folk combined, there wasn't much chance of that. She ignored the stares as she walked in with Bryan a few minutes before the service was to start. He entered a pew, followed by Lauren and the boys. On the other end of the row Dirk adjusted his new cardboard dad as the organist quietly played the strains of *Oh Little Town of Bethlehem* as people filled the chapel.

"You don't mind that, do you?" Lauren asked.

"We've got to make sure this family is well protected, with a guy on either end of the row." He smiled and whispered, "Besides, I hear one of them is the type who only goes to church on Easter and Christmas."

"Do you think that will ever change?"

"He's cardboard. I think you could bring him every week and he wouldn't put up much of a fight." He gave her hand a little squeeze. "I've had more than a few prayers answered recently, so sure, count me in. Make my sister a happy woman. And my mom and dear departed dad, my cousins, nieces and nephews. I come from a long line of religious addicts. It was just a matter of time before I got sucked back in."

They hurried out of the church building after the services. "Under the circumstances, I really don't want to talk to anyone," she told him. Then she looked up and saw Charlene standing alone, facing away from the building, probably waiting for her husband to bring the car around. "Well, maybe there's one person I need to talk to."

Bryan stayed with the boys, watching the two women hug and say whatever each of them felt needed to be said. Dirk tugged at Bryan's suit jacket.

"How long is Mommy gonna talk? We wanna go home and play with our toys."

"I hear ya, buddy. Oh look, here she comes now. Think of this. Next time Christmas comes on a Sunday will be several years from now. Church is done, and now you get to play with your toys the rest of the day."

Bryan reached down and picked up Lauren's youngest son.

"Toys," said Brett. "Toys."

It surprised Bryan how the little guy saying one new word was so exciting for him. He waved Lauren over. "Tell Mommy your new word."

"Toys," Brett said again.

Lauren reached over and zipped up his coat. "An appropriate word for the day."

"It is. So we'd best be on our way and reinforce the meaning of that word," Bryan said.

Back at the house the boys begged to change out of their vests and bowties. "We can't change clothes, guys. We're going to Grampa and Grammy's house for dinner and everybody gets dressed up, even when Christmas *isn't* on a Sunday. But remember that all your cousins will be there."

"Michael and Danny?"

"Yes, they'll be there."

Dirk turned to Bryan. "Grammy has the coolest basement you ever saw. She has books all over and blocks and she has a room with a Lego table. When we make stuff, Grammy has a special shelf and she lets us each keep one thing there that nobody can take apart except us. It has our name by it. And she says when I get older, she's going to give me all of my dad's old Legos."

"Now that sounds like a very cool grandma."

195

"Are you coming to our grandma's house, Bryan?"

"Oh no, I'm headed over to my sister's house for dinner."

"You *could* come, if you wanted," Lauren said tentatively. "Janet is kind of a the-more-the-merrier type. She always overcooks. I already called and asked if she minded if I brought three other people. She said to round up all the strays I wanted and come on over."

"What three people?"

"You would know them as Amber, Marie and Katie. They're here in town and didn't have anywhere to go."

"How did you know how to contact them?"

"I have my sources," she said.

"Believe me, Lauren, I would love nothing more than to spend the entire day in your company." *My entire life, for that matter.* "But wouldn't that be kind of awkward for you . . . and for them?"

She held up her left hand. He could see that the ring that had been there the day before was no longer on her finger. She smiled and pulled a gold chain out from under her blouse. Dangling from it was her wedding rings. "Kind of like Cardboard Kendall, for as long as I need them."

He took her by the hand, stroking the empty finger, contemplating that if things worked out the way he hoped they would, it wouldn't always be bare. He spoke softly. "I'd love to spend the day with you, but it could be hurtful for them to see you with someone else, and that's the last thing I'd want to do to someone on Christmas Day."

"I promised the Michigan ladies that I'd find a ride for them. I was just going to send one of Kendall's brothers to pick them up at the Holiday Inn on Broadway. What if you picked them up and just came along as the guy who had a part in reuniting a mother with her daughters?"

"A poor lonely beggar with no one in the world to be with on Christmas?"

"If the boot fits, Santa . . ."

"Hmmmm. Three more women in my truck . . . Okay, let me call Samantha. She's actually kind of a the-fewer-the-merrier type, but even if she wasn't, I think she'd give me her blessing to duck out in favor of such an invitation. I'm sure she'll gladly take my plate off the table. Her idea of an ideal Christmas is being with her husband and their three kids. Our mother retired to Arizona near our brother in Mesa and has absolutely no interest of visiting any of us in the dead of winter, least of all my oldest brother in Montana."

"So, you're in?"

"Okay, you talked me into it, if you think you can keep your hands off me for a few hours."

"As long as songs about kissing Santa don't come on the radio, I think I can control myself."

"Sami warned me that this new aftershave would make me irresistible to women."

"What's it called?"

"Scintillating Santa."

"Sure it is."

"Okay, it's *Old Spice*. But please don't tell Sami."

"You might be the one who keeps her from winning the cruise," Lauren said.

"No chance of that, even with all the lipsticks she took back from Charlene on credit. She's milking the press. Haven't you seen the paper yet? Sami's big news. The headline says, 'Little White Lie Cracks Big Case.'"

"I haven't looked at the paper. Personally, I don't want to know they've said about my involvement in any of it. I'm just hoping we can put it all behind us."

"Sami figures it'll probably bring in more business, in case there is someone left in Colorado who isn't already buying from her. You should have seen her at work this month. She put together sample gift packages in all price ranges for both sexes and went around to lazy businessmen all over the greater Denver area taking orders to simplify their corporate and personal gift giving. She had to borrow my truck for all her deliveries, so I made my contribution in wear and tear on my vehicle, not to mention I bought a tarp. Just remember, if you dump me, there are three women in Boulder known to be in possession of *Peppermint*

197

Passion lipsticks and being a police sergeant, I can find their addresses."

"Do what ya gotta do, Sergeant."

"Sami's just waiting for them to tally up the totals for the year, but she's already bought three new tropical bathing suits, or so my brother-in-law reports. She'll have a jump on next year when I hold my Pre-Superbowl Party where she's going to talk about the virtues of exfoliating to my fellow officers and friends. I owe her now, and I'm sure that's going to be the price I pay."

Lauren laughed. "Sounds like fun." She switched gears. "I think I can resist you in *Old Spice*. That's what my grandpa used to wear."

"Don't speak too soon, sistah. Haven't you seen the commercials? This is *not* your grandpa's *Old Spice.*"

* * *

Janet Baylor warmly welcomed the trio of ladies—Marisol, Hannah, and Elizabeth, and their escort, Sergeant Everett. Janet didn't miss the look that passed between Lauren and the police sergeant when he arrived. The girls' eyes lit up when they saw Lauren and there were hugs all around. A tear came to her eye as Lauren realized that maybe her children weren't the ones who had been traumatized the most this holiday season. Hannah and Lizzie were immediately whisked away to the basement by Dirk and a couple of his cousins.

"I hope they're going to be okay," Lauren said to their mother.

"I can't imagine how horrible it must have been for you to be separated from your children," Janet said.

"We're taking things a day at a time. Thank heavens we've got Christmas as a diversion. We'll get down to the serious business of healing starting tomorrow." She grasped Janet's hand. "You have been so gracious to take us in."

"Oh heavens! Our friends and family are dear to us, even people like you who might only be in our lives for a day."

Tears sprang to Marisol's eyes. "I was so glad to hear that while my girls were away from me they were often in the care of your kind daughter-in-law. Phillip, my ex-husband, could be a

198

good father sometimes, but he had a mean streak, and he could be very controlling. I worried every day about what was happening to my daughters and prayed that if they were still alive, somehow they would fall into the hands of kind strangers along the way."

Lauren spoke up. "When Lloyd—Phillip—told me that their mother hadn't sent them any Christmas presents, I said to myself that it was unbelievable, that I couldn't believe a mother wouldn't care enough to send something to her little girls. There were always little lingering doubts I had about him, no matter how much I tried to quiet them. I realize now that it bothered me because it really *was* unbelievable, at least in this case. I couldn't truly believe that a mother would just leave her daughters without a backward glance." Lauren looked down at Brett who was staying close to her and trying to avoid a couple of overzealous girl cousins about his age.

"I'm curious," Marisol asked. "Why *did* I do it?"

"Oh, you were a wealthy career woman and . . ." Lauren steered Marisol over to a couple of wingback chairs in the corner. She hoisted Brett up onto her lap and put a protective arm around him. It warmed Bryan's heart to hear their laughter, and he left them alone to commiserate and compare notes about the man who had brought them both so much grief. The more they talked, the more Marisol's English took on a Spanish accent and her grammar slipped into a more casual style.

"Career woman? Phillip didn't let me work anywhere. It threaten his manhood. He told me he was going to make us rich beyond my wildest dreams. I don't know he means he do it by stealing."

"So did he make all that up, working at Motorola, south Florida?"

"Motorola close the plant in Boynton Beach in 2004, so he work there until then. I grew up in Miami, so we were close to my family, but we move to Detroit when he found work there at General Motors as an engineer," Marisol said.

"I have another question. Something about Barbie dolls and you not wanting the girls to have them. Bryan got me thinking about that and all through this all I've been trying to figure out how the Barbie dolls fit in."

"Oh, I never want my girls to have Barbie dolls. I don't think she is a good role model."

Lauren laughed. "If Barbie had that much influence, ninety-nine percent of the little girls in this country would be messed up."

Marisol was beginning to feel comfortable around these people and started to loosen up even more. She leaned over and whispered to Lauren. "I think Barbie is a *skank.*" She returned to a regular conversational tone. "Going around with her big blond hair and hooker shoes, in her mini-skirt trying to get Ken's attention with her big Barbie boob job." Marisol did her best impression of Barbie. "Oh Kennn . . ." She batted her eyelashes and beckoned with her index finger.

Lauren set her glass on a nearby table, laughing and placing her open hand on her chest. "You're going to make me choke on my eggnog."

Marisol was just warming up. "What kind of man is Ken with his little plastic hair?"

"Ken *is* kind of in Barbie's shadow, isn't he?" Lauren commented. "My husband's name was Kendall and Ken Doll was his nickname all through high school."

"Ken, he doesn't have a job. I think he lives in Barbie's dream house and drives her pink Corvette and looks at himself in the mirror a lot." She laughed heartily. "In Miami, my friends, we call all the blond girls with big poufy hair Barbies. I have always thought she was a spoiled stuck-up rich girl. There was a blond girl in my high school who was mean to me, so I never liked Barbie after that. No. No Barbies for my girls."

"I get it now," Lauren said. "Lloyd tried to paint a certain picture of you and you being a mother who cared about whether or not a doll was a good role model didn't fit, because he . . . hadn't exactly painted *you* out to be the world's best role model."

"I can only imagine the things he told you about me." She batted her eyelashes again. "Am I a Barbie?" She doubled over laughing at her own joke. "When the judge gave us joint custody,

Phillip was not happy. He likes to be the boss. He doesn't share well."

From across the room, Bryan piped up. "I noticed that."

"Because he shared custody, he was able to sign them out of school. Nobody thought anything was wrong. I guess when he find out the car company know he was stealing, he decide to take our daughters, too, and leave town. He took them at the beginning of the day, so by the time school was out that day and I realized the girls were gone and he had taken them, he'd had over six hours to get out of town and cover his tracks. When the FBI find out about the things he stole from the car company, they think I must know something, until they realize he take my girls."

"I don't know how you survived that," Lauren said.

"I didn't even know about his step-sister in Colorado. He couldn't access the money or that would have led them right to him, so he had to find a way to survive in the meantime. The only thing that kept me going was that I believe in his own mixed-up way he loves the girls and I believe he wouldn't hurt them. To survive, I had to try to tell myself they were somewhere being loved and cared for. If you will tell me how to call her, I would like to also thank his sister. She didn't know what he was doing, and I'm sure she was kind to my daughters, like you were."

"That would mean a lot to her. I know she feels responsible somehow, and it would help a lot to know that you don't blame her for hiding him," Lauren said. "So many things make sense now, like why he was staying with his former step-sister, someone who was probably off the radar, especially since his mother had been married three times."

"I didn't even know she existed," Marisol said. "Phillip thought he could write the rules the way he wanted to live them. I'm still trying to figure out how to talk to the girls about all of this. First, I'm sure their father told them terrible things about me and things that weren't true. Now I'm trying not to return the favor and tell them horrible things about him. They know that he lied to them when he took them from their school that day and that he has been lying about everything ever since. His actions are speaking for themselves. And I wish he hadn't been wearing a Santa suit when they arrested him. This is not good for my girls."

"Maybe we can get some group therapy for our kids. You wouldn't believe how many messed-up stories I have from these two men in Santa suits trying to romance me," Lauren said, hoping Janet was still in the kitchen.

"I *should* move here. We can be best friends. You're a little bit Barbie, but not *too* much, even if you were married to Ken Doll. Phillip, he's like a big bellowing moose if someone is in his territory. When I met him, I thought he was handsome and successful and charming, but as soon as we were married, he wanted to control everything I did. It is funny because I did not want to marry some macho Spanish guy, so I marry a controlling white guy instead. I will probably move back to Florida to be close to my family. Maybe you can bring your boys on vacation and we can go to Disney World."

She picked up a frosted sugar cookie off her snack plate. "Maybe I find a nice Spanish guy who likes my cooking and isn't too macho. I will find him at Disney World in Cinderella castle with all the other imaginary creatures." She laughed again. "Phillip, he never like my Latin cooking. He had a *delicate stomach*, never want anything with spice in it."

Lauren grabbed her arm. "I have to tell you about the vision he had from my dead husband . . ."

As the two ladies swapped stories and laughed in the corner, the introverted Sergeant Everett uncomfortably found himself the sole object of Janet Baylor's scrutiny. She took him by the arm and led him to the small sofa near where her husband sat, comfortably stretched out in a black leather lounge chair, head bobbing.

"Dinner won't be on for a bit." She picked up a nearby box of chocolates. "Have a chocolate." He reached in and came back with a caramel. "So you're the Santa who bought that special gift for my grandson, replaced the cardboard daddy that took a bath." Her eyes misted up. "Such a contrast to that other fellow's behavior. Why if I could get my hands on him . . ."

202

Lauren looked over from her corner, overhearing her mother-in-law, wondering why it was Janet and not her husband talking like this. Usually it was the men ready to form a lynch mob. She looked at her father-in-law. Bob nodded silently in the background, stirring awake when he heard his wife's voice raised. Lauren was sure he felt no less passionate about it all, but he had always been a man of few words.

Lauren looked at solemn little Brett on her lap. Then back at Bob. Back to Brett. "Bob!" The word exploded from her. "He's like you!"

"Hmmm? What?" he asked, jarring awake.

"Brett! There's nothing wrong with him! He's the strong silent type, a man of few words. Falls asleep at the drop of a hat. I don't know why I didn't see this before! He even looks like you. He's a little carbon copy of his grandfather."

Bob smiled and nodded. "Hmmph. Could be." Then his head slumped back down on his chest and he was out.

Janet laughed. "I've known that all along, Lauren. What took you so long?"

She turned her attention back to Bryan. "So anyway, I want to thank you for what you did for my grandson."

"I take very little credit. Usually those photo reproductions take longer but when you put a bunch of sentimental ladies to work on something, miracles happen."

"Never underestimate women on a mission, certainly, but, oh yes, you deserve credit. It demonstrates what kind of a man you are, showing compassion for a little boy and showing respect for my son. Those are a couple of pretty important things to a grandmother and a mother."

Lauren had paused in her conversation long enough to eavesdrop on their exchange. "She's right, you know. You're the one who taught me that the evidence doesn't lie."

Janet waited for a lull in the conversation before she recruited Lauren's help to assist her in removing the turkey from the oven. She set down her oven mitt on the counter and cut off a little piece of turkey, handing a small bite to Lauren. "Done to perfection, wouldn't you say?"

Lauren waited to swallow before she answered. "I won't argue with that."

"When you've done as many turkeys as I have, you finally learn all the tricks," Janet said.

"I've been reading this great book called *Speedbumps* by Teri Garr. In it she said her grandmother used to say 'Ve get too soon old und too late schmart.'"

"Ain't that the truth! Sounds like a good book."

"And her mother used to tell her EGBOK, which stand for Everything is Going to Be Okay. I've been repeating that to myself a lot lately."

"In spite of everything, I think we're *all* going to be okay." She reached a large casserole dish out of the cupboard. "By the way, I want you to know I approve."

"You *approve*?" ask Lauren.

"Of the sergeant. No need to be coy. You think I was born yesterday? I can see how he lights up when you're within ten feet of him, and I don't want to embarrass you, but these walls aren't that thick." She hugged her daughter-in-law and then held her at arm's length and smiled. "I see some light back in your eyes. I can't think of a better Christmas gift than that."

Lauren smiled. "We're just starting to get acquainted, which might be a little easier with all this out of the way, but maybe you're right. After all, as they say, the evidence doesn't lie."

A few minutes later they all sat around the dining room table enjoying Christmas dinner. Janet paused, her fork poised in the air, and looked at Bryan. "So Sergeant . . . a tale of two Santas. Have you ever thought of writing a book?"

"No one would believe it," he said.

"You're probably right about that." She looked between Bryan and her daughter-in-law. Janet looked Bryan square in the eye and gave him a little wink. "Well, if you ever do write it, Sergeant Everett, for all our sakes, make sure it has a happy ending."

Other books by Susan Law Corpany

Brotherly Love
Unfinished Business
Push On
Are We There Yet?
Lucky Change
A Beacon Light
Running the River of Life
Musings on Motherhood

**Available at amazon.com
or by contacting the author at <u>susancorpany@aol.com</u>**

Visit the author's blogs:

http://Paradisepromotions.blogspot.com

http://akazillionactsofservice.blogspot.com

http://templetravelingtigger.blogspot.com

http://thecomicreliefsociety.blogspot.com

vrbo.com/109651 (Our vacation rental home)

Author Susan Law Corpany and Crew

Made in the USA
Las Vegas, NV
18 November 2023

81116884R00118